glamorous Beaded Jewelry

BRACELETS, NECKLACES, EARRINGS, AND RINGS

glamorous
Beaded Jewelry

BRACELETS, NECKLACES, EARRINGS, AND RINGS

M. T. Ryan

CREATIVE HOMEOWNER®, Upper Saddle River, New Jersey

GLAMOROUS BEADED JEWELRY

SENIOR EDITOR: Carol Sterbenz
SENIOR DESIGNER: Glee Barre
DESIGNERS: Amanda Wilson, Stephanie Phelan
ASSISTANT EDITOR: Evan Lambert
TECHNICAL EDITORS: Candie Frankel, Emily Harste, Marilyn Knowlton
PHOTO RESEARCHER: Robyn Poplasky
INDEXER: Schroeder Indexing Services
PRINCIPAL PHOTOGRAPHY: Steven Mays
INSTRUCTIONAL PHOTOGRAPHY: M. T. Ryan and Steven Mays
PATTERNS AND ORIGINAL ART: Marta Curry and Roberta Frauwirth
DIAGRAMS: Diane P. Smith-Gale

CREATIVE HOMEOWNER

VP/PUBLISHER: Brian Toolan
VP/EDITORIAL DIRECTOR: Timothy O. Bakke
PRODUCTION MANAGER: Kimberly H. Vivas
ART DIRECTOR: David Geer
MANAGING EDITOR: Fran J. Donegan

Printed in China

Current Printing (last digit)
10 9 8 7 6 5 4 3 2 1

Glamorous Beaded Jewelry, First Edition
Library of Congress Control Number: 2005933623
ISBN-10: 1-58011-295-1
ISBN-13: 978-1-58011-295-6

CREATIVE HOMEOWNER®
A Division of Federal Marketing Corp.
24 Park Way
Upper Saddle River, NJ 07458
www.creativehomeowner.com

Dedication

For Micko & Dave

Acknowledgments

Thanks go to Carol Endler Sterbenz, whose inspiration and support made this book possible. Thanks also to Glee Barre, Senior Designer, Amanda Wilson, Stephanie Phelan, and Diane P. Smith-Gale who made the pages of the work beautiful; to Evan Lambert, Assistant Editor; to Candie Frankel, Emily Harste, and Marilyn Knowlton, superb technical editors all; and to Steven Mays for the stunning photography.

CONTENTS

Introduction

BEADED JEWELRY has evolved far beyond simple stringing, and the looks are much more glamorous and varied than ever before. In *Glamorous Beaded Jewelry* you are presented with 25 fun yet sophisticated pieces of jewelry that range in sprit from elegant simplicity to richly layered designs using unexpected combinations of semiprecious stones. But just because a piece of beaded jewelry looks expensive or hard to make doesn't mean that it is. Achieving a satisfying crafting outcome is about choosing materials carefully and about taking advantage of the relatively new methods—like crimping—and novel materials—like dyed quartz that simulates much more expensive stones—now available.

In *Glamorous Beaded Jewelry*, you will be guided to near professional-looking results with the creation of each stunning piece of jewelry. Clear step-by-step directions are accompanied by helpful diagrams and gorgeous color photography that captures every sparkling detail of each original. You can create variations of the featured designs, or you can use your imagination and the fundamental beading techniques to create designs to suit your very own style.

M T Ryan

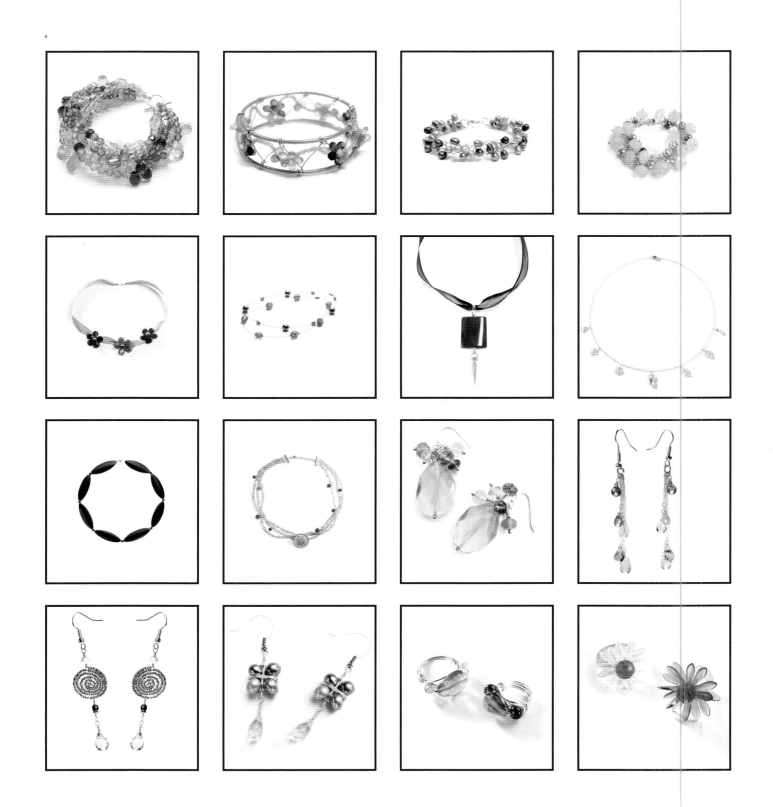

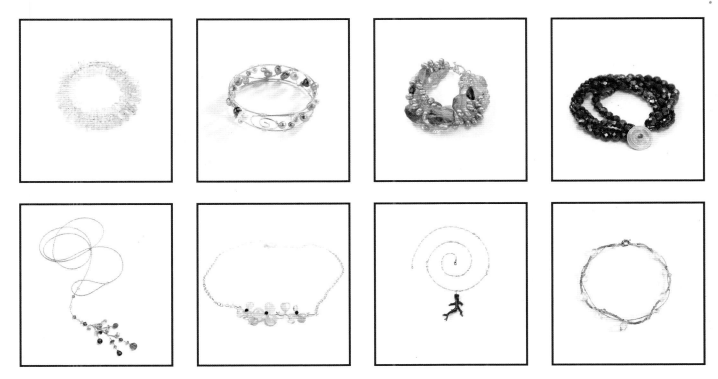

The Collection

"The Collection" features a sparkling array of bracelets,

necklaces, rings, and earrings, each designed

with imagination and style, using beads of every description.

Whether you are looking for an elegant pendant, a bracelet

made of chunky beads in candy colors, or a necklace made

from lustrous gold nuggets, Glamorous Beaded Jewelry will

show you how to make each signature piece.

mix smooth and chunky
beads for a fun look

Pink Ice

Big splashes of color can be achieved from small beads when single strands are loosely braided together. To add more textural interest and sparkle, mix in large chunky beads in oval, round, and disk shapes, including beads with two-tone or metallic lusters. The variety of beads will produce a bracelet with shimmering color and movement.

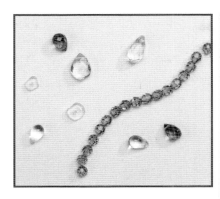

MATERIALS

- 5 crystal briolettes, faceted, in pale pink, 12mm long x 9mm wide x 5mm thick
- 13 crystal teardrop beads, faceted, in yellow, 2mm long x 7mm wide
- 7 crystal flat beads, disk-shaped with faceted edges, in red, 6mm dia. x 3mm thick
- 4 round glass beads, in pink/green, 8mm dia.
- 4 round beads, faceted, in clear pink/metallic, 5mm dia.
- 5 tube beads, faceted, in pale pink, 12mm long x 6mm dia.
- 3 glass teardrop beads, in clear pink, 9mm long x 5mm wide
- 8 glass chips, in milky pink, 8mm dia. x 2mm thick
- 10 teardrop beads, faceted, in violet 9mm long x 5mm wide
- 6 pink seed beads, 6/0
- 2 pink seed beads 10/0
- 159 cut crystal round beads, 5mm dia.: 52 light rose, 57 rose, and 50 deep rose
- Tigertail
- 12 silver crimp tubes, size 1

TOOLS

- Wire cutters ■ Needle-nose pliers
- Crimping tool ■ Safety goggles
- Paper tissues

●●● Making a Pink Ice Bracelet

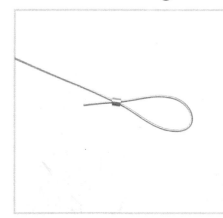

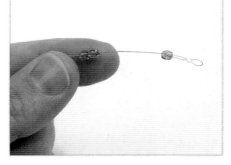

1 Cut six 8-in. lengths of tigertail using the wire cutters. Insert the end of one strand into a crimp tube. Fold over ½ in. and insert the tip back into the tube to form a ⅛-in.- diameter loop. Use the crimping tool to squash the crimp tube to secure the loop. Prepare the remaining lengths of tigertail in the same way.

2 Following the beading diagram, string the beads on the first strand. Tuck the loose tail at the crimp tube into the first two beads to conceal it. Continue beading until the strand is fully loaded and 1 in. of the tigertail remains. Add a seed bead to the end as a temporary spacer.

3 To end the strand, thread on a crimp tube. Hold the strand vertically using the tip of the needle-nose pliers so that all the beads slide down as far as possible. Fold over the tigertail, and insert the tip back into the tube. Slide the tube down until only a ⅛-in. loop of tigertail remains. Squash the crimp tube using the crimping tool. Repeat steps 1–3 to string the beads on the remaining five strands.

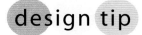

An ombre effect is created by graduating the color of the beads from strand to strand, going from light to dark. The effect produces the appearance of glowing gradient color. When the larger beads are placed within the strands, they add extra shots of color and sparkle.

4 Put on the safety goggles. Wrap a folded tissue around the last seed bead and crush it using the throat of the needle-nose pliers.* Discard the tissue. Repeat for each beaded strand.

*Note: the removal of this bead will provide just enough space to keep the bracelet flexible.

5 Lay the beaded strands on a flat surface, arranging them by color from light rose to dark rose. Thread the loops at one end on an open jump ring, using the pliers to close the ring when finished.

6 Use the pliers to thread an open jump ring through the loop on the bar part of the toggle clasp and the jump ring that holds the beaded strands affixed in step 5. Close the ring. Arrange the strands in a loose braid. Use a new open jump ring to connect the free loops and the ring part of the clasp.

diagram

KEY FOR BASE BEADS: a. light rose cut crystal round beads **b.** rose cut crystal round beads **c.** deep rose cut crystal round beads
KEY FOR BEAD ACCENTS: 1. Pale pink faceted briolette **2.** Yellow faceted teardrop beads **3.** Red disk-shaped flat bead with faceted edge **4.** Pink/green round glass bead **5.** Clear pink/metallic faceted round bead **6.** Pale pink faceted tube bead **7.** Milky pink glass chips **8.** Violet faceted teardrop beads **9.** Pink clear glass smooth teardrop beads

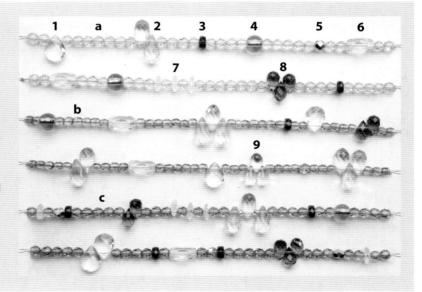

a garland winds through

Violet Garland Bangle

The secret to this delicate bracelet is the intriguing way it is made.

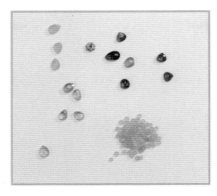

The foundation is formed by lashing together two store-bought bangle bracelets using matching wire. Each wire "stitch" connects the bangles, forming a graceful diagonal pattern that encircles the cuff. A delicate vine of violets, reminiscent of a trellis of spring flowers, is woven into the cuff.

golden **hoops**

MATERIALS

- *To make the cuff:*

  2 gold-tone bangle bracelets, 2½" dia., 12-gauge round wire

  3 wooden beads, ¾" dia.

  Brass wire, 22-gauge

- *To decorate the cuff:*

  46 crystal briolettes, flat, pear-shaped, 7mm long x 5mm wide x 2mm thick:

  > *20 assorted purple, violet, and pink*

  > *20 pink*

  > *8 kelly green*

  > *6 milky mint green*

  8 gold spacer beads, florette style, 5mm dia. x 1mm thick

  8 white seed pearls, 2mm dia.

  1 vial lime green seed beads, satin finish, 12/0

  Transite

  Brass wire, 24-gauge

TOOLS

Wire cutters ■ Needle-nose pliers ■ Hook-nose pliers ■ Emery cloth ■ Thread scissors ■ Permanent felt tip marker ■ Beading glue ■ Crimper tool ■ Ruler ■ Safety goggles

•••• Making a Violet Garland Bracelet

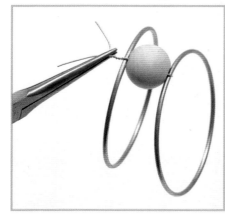

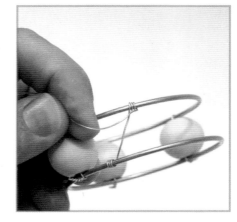

1 Put on safety goggles. Fold a 2-in.
length of brass wire in half around a
bangle. Slip on a wooden spacer bead. Trap
the second bangle between the wire ends,
and twist to tighten using needle-nose
pliers. Repeat with the other two wooden
beads, dividing the bangle into thirds.

2 Smooth one end of a 42-in. length of
wire with emery cloth. Lap one end of
the wire under one bangle by ¹/₂ in. Use
pliers to wind the wire end around the bangle. Pull the wire sideways at a 45-degree
angle. Wind it over and around the second
bangle three times, then around the diagonal wire. Pull toward you, cinching tightly.

3 Pull the wire at a 45-degree angle
toward the first bangle. Wrap it three
times and cinch it, as in step 2. Repeat this
zigzag pattern around the circumference,
sliding the balls aside slowly as you work.
Snip off and remove the balls, one by one,
to make space for the final wraps.

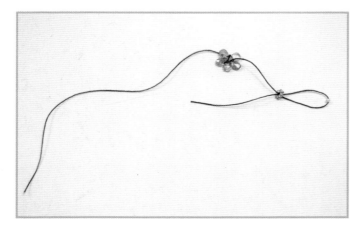

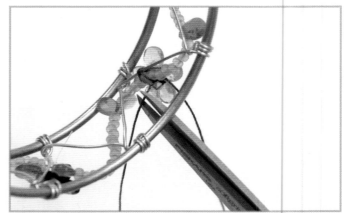

7 Cut a 12-in. length of transite, and mark a point ¹/₂ in. from one
end. Thread on 5 pink quartz beads. Tie a square knot, drawing
the beads into a flower-shaped cluster. Bring one end of the transite
up through the flower center. Slip on a daisy spacer bead and a seed
bead, and thread the transite back through the spacer bead and into
the flower cluster.

8 Place a flower on the bracelet where the garland crosses the
diagonal brass wire. Tie the transite strands in a square knot on
the inside of the bracelet. On the right side, tie another square knot
at the base of the flower behind its petals. Secure this knot with
beading glue and let it dry. Trim off the excess transite. Repeat to
attach each flower.

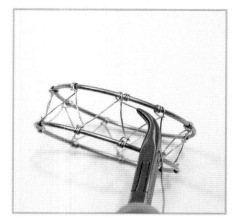  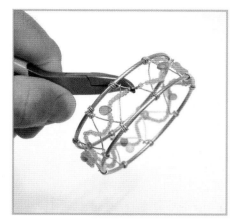

4 Connect the wire diagonally to the starting point, sliding the wire loops forward or backward around the circumference so that the triangles are even. You should have nine winding knots on each bangle. Cinch the joint, and cut off the excess wire. Gently press and flatten each wire wrap with pliers to prevent shifting.

5 Cut an 11-in. length of 24-gauge brass wire. Attach a crimp bead to one end, leaving a ½-in. tail unbeaded. Thread green seed beads onto the wire for ½ in.; then add one or two green quartz beads. Continue stringing beads until there are ten "leaf" clusters spaced 1 in. apart. End with ½ in. of seed beads and a crimp bead.

6 Bend the beaded strand by hand every ¾ in. or so to form a wavy strip. Wrap the "garland" around the cuff, and position the strip so that the seed bead sections of the garland cross over the wire zigzags. Overlap the ends.

diagram

The "leafy garland" is made from one strand of wire that is beaded with seed beads and glass chips. Use the diagram to guide the placement of your beads, or improvise by adding more leaves if you desire. Leave a ½-in. section of wire unbeaded at the beginning and end of the strand in order to wire the garland to the cuff. Thereafter, attach the violets to key points to secure the garland to the cuff.

Crimp bead … Crimp bead
Tail … Tail
½" ½" … ½" ½"

Important Measurements:

11 in. The length of the wire strand

10 in. The length of the garland from crimp bead to crimp bead

1 in. The space between the leaves

½ in. The unbeaded tails of wire at the beginning and end of the garland

iridescent pearls tumble in a frothy web

Pastel Pearl Meringue

Crochet can be used to create beautiful wire jewelry. Borrowed

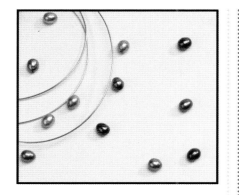

from needlework, the technique is not difficult to master once you get the feel for working with hard wire instead of pliable yarn. Fortunately, the crocheted loops in this bracelet don't need to be perfectly formed, as their irregular character helps to create the unexpected beauty in the band of wire filigree.

MATERIALS

- 47 oval freshwater pearls, 6mm long x 5mm dia., in assorted colors:
  - 2 purple
  - 3 taupe
  - 5 soft pink
  - 5 copper
  - 5 bronze
  - 8 gunmetal gray
  - 9 champagne
  - 10 lime green
- Gold-plated wire, 24-gauge
- Gold-plated lobster-claw clasp
- Gold plated open jump ring, 4mm dia.

TOOLS

- Wire cutters ■ Hook-nose pliers
- Optional: crochet hook, US size 7 (1.5mm)

21

Making a Pastel Pearl Meringue Bracelet

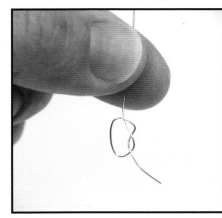

1 To make the crocheted base of the bracelet, begin by cutting a 36-in. length of 24-gauge gold wire. Make a simple slipknot having a 1/4-in. diameter, leaving a 1/2-in. tail.

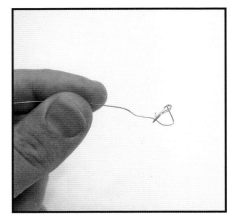

2 Form the loose wire near the knot into a 1/4-in. diameter loop. Push the new loop through the slip knot. If necessary, use the crochet hook to pull the loop through. Shape the loop into an upside-down teardrop using your fingers.

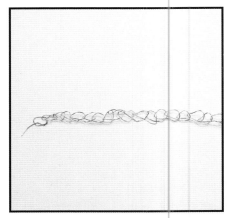

3 Repeat step 2 to make a new loop in each previous loop. Continue until the band is 7 in. long. Thread the wire end through the last loop, and pull it taut. Snip off the remaining wire using wire cutters, leaving a 1/2-in. tail.

7 Wrap the 1/2-in. wire tails around the end loop on opposite sides, using the hook-nose pliers to ensure a tight wrap. Repeat the step to wrap the wire tails around the end loop at the other end of the band.

Fixing Kinks

Kinks in wire are easy to fix. Gently open up the kink and straighten the wire between the jaws of a pair of pliers. As an added measure, place the fixed kink section of wire on a flat surface and rub over the spot using an orange stick.

8 Attach a lobster claw clasp to one end loop, using a small jump ring. To style the crocheted wire, lightly scrunch the loops between your fingers. Then twist gently on the pearls to raise them up slightly so they resemble offset buds.

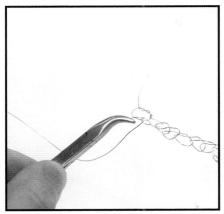

4 To decorate the band, begin by lining up the loose pearls in a random order of color. If the pearls are already strung randomly by color, as these are, pick them off one at a time as you work.

5 Cut a 36-in. length of gold wire, and fasten one end to the crocheted band at one end. Thread the opposite end through the first pearl. Slide the pearl down to the band until it emerges at the back side, leaving a loose loop with the pearl on the front side. Scrunch down the pearl with your thumb.

6 Run the wire back through the band, zigzagging to the other edge. Thread on another pearl and place it about $\frac{1}{8}$ in. from the first. Scrunch the wire and position the pearl so it is near, but not touching, the first pearl. Repeat the steps until the band is decorated in a random pattern of pearls. After the last pearl, pull the wire through the end loop of the crocheted base and wrap it until only a $\frac{1}{2}$-in. tail remains.

design tip

Instead of using all of the pearl colors that come on a single strand of assorted colors, make several bracelets, using only one color on each. Then, stack the bracelets on your wrist bangle-style.

mix melon-colored beads

Honeydew Cluster

This bracelet is about carefully modulated contrasts—the icy cool minty greens of the jadite stones with their sparkling facets, and the exotic jewel tones of the lustrous dyed pearls. The exquisitely chunky bracelet is fairly heavy, but the double-link chain helps support the beads, and a lobster-claw clasp and extra-thick jump ring help ensure completely beautiful and worry-free wear.

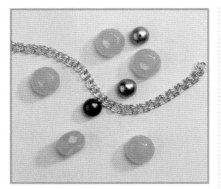

MATERIALS

- 19 rondelles, faceted, dyed quartz beads:

    16 milky green jadite, 12mm dia. x 8mm thick

    3 milky dark jadite, 15mm dia. x 11mm thick

- 15 assorted freshwater pearls, 8mm dia. x 6mm thick:

    4 copper

    6 pale bronze

    3 moss green

    2 natural white

- 16 sterling silver ball-head pins, 2" long, 18-gauge

- 7-in. sterling silver double-round-link chain, 4mm dia. links, 16-gauge wire

- 1 sterling silver lobster-claw clasp closure

- 1 sterling silver heavy closed jump ring, 6mm dia., 12-gauge

- Silver wire, 28-gauge

- 15 white seed pearls, 1mm to 1.5mm dia.

TOOLS:
- Needle-nose pliers ■ Wire snips

Making a Honeydew Cluster Bracelet

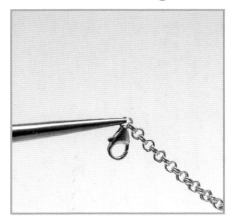

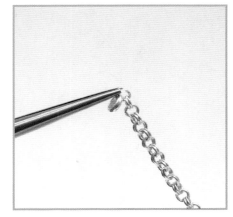

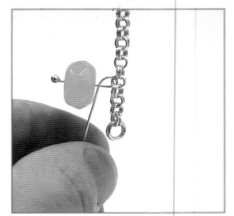

1 Connect the lobster-claw clasp to one end of the chain using an open jump ring. Close the ring using the needle-nose pliers.

2 Connect a closed jump ring to the other end of the chain using a second, smaller open jump ring, and using the pliers to close it neatly and securely.

3 Insert a head pin into one of the smaller rondelle beads. Make a crook about $^3/_{16}$ in. above the bead using the pliers. Bend the wire into a loop. Before closing the loop and winding its stem, thread the end tail through the fourth link from the jump ring at one end of the chain.

7 Repeat step 6 to attach the remaining 14 pearls, filling in all 15 gaps between the 16 rondelle beads, referring to the color diagram at right.

diagram

Key to beads:

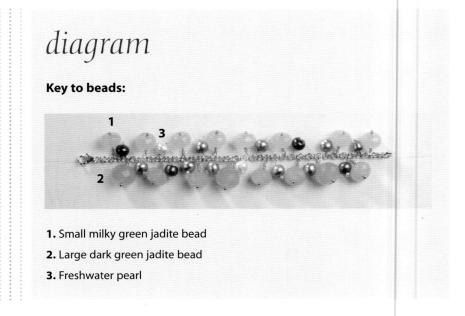

1. Small milky green jadite bead

2. Large dark green jadite bead

3. Freshwater pearl

 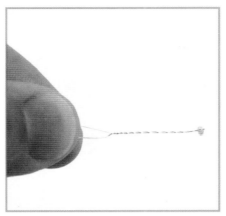 

4 Insert a head pin into a larger rondelle bead. Make a crook about ¼ in. above the bead. Follow step 3 to attach the rondelle bead to the eighth link in the chain. Attach the remaining beads at four-link intervals, leaving 3 links free at each end.

5 Cut a 3-in. length of 28-gauge wire. Fold it in half, trapping a seed pearl in the fold. Roll the pearl between your fingers on one hand, and with the fingers on the other hand, twist the wires into a single stem. Repeat to make 15 seed pearl "head pins".

6 Insert a pearl head pin into one pearl. Thread the wire end into the chain link exactly halfway between the first and second rondelle beads. Make a crook ³⁄₁₆ in. above the pearl. Wrap the wire tail around the stem until the pearl is secure. Then snip off any excess wire using the wire snips.

design tip

For a stylish alternative, mix chunky crystal beads in water-clear blue and large faceted rondelles in the palest apricot and persimmon.

hoops of pink beads create a
pretty ruffle

Slinky Cuff

The underlying key to the soft "petals" of this bracelet is springy

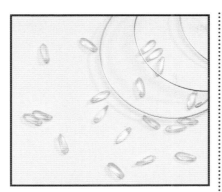

steel wire. Bent into hoops and threaded with slender dagger beads, the wire cuff surrounds the wrist in a ruffle of pale color. Seed beads are interspersed among the dagger beads so that the dagger beads can swivel freely around the wire core, creating movement when the cuff is worn, and lending playful sophistication.

MATERIALS

■ 186 dagger beads, 9mm long:

    1 pkg. or 62 beads in clear pink

    1 pkg. or 62 beads in frosted pink

    1 pkg. or 62 iridescent beads in frosted pink

■ 185 seed beads in pink with mirrored centers, 10/0

■ 1 spool of memory wire in bright silver, large bracelet weight

TOOLS

■ Wire cutters ■ Needle-nose pliers
■ Emery cloth ■ Protective goggles

●●● Making a Slinky Cuff Bracelet

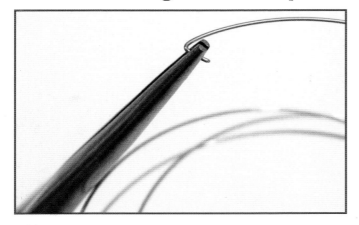

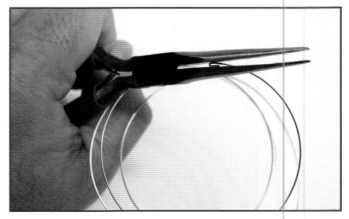

1 Unspool four turns of memory wire, and cut the length, using the wire cutters. Smooth the cut ends with emery cloth. At one end, use the tip of the needle-nose pliers to bend a ⅛-in. length into an L-shape.

2 Use the throat section of the pliers to squeeze the bend until it flattens neatly against the wire. Note: this fold will keep the beads from sliding off and the wire from snagging clothing when the bracelet is worn.

design tip

The roughly four turns of wire
shown here will stack enough petals or
dagger beads to create a suitably
fluffy cuff. For a more delicate look, use
a shorter length of wire.
For a denser, heavier look, use a longer
wire to create more coils.

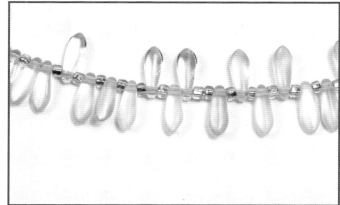

3 Mix the three colors of dagger beads in a small tin or dish. Put on safety goggles, as wire has tendency to swing. Thread the straight end of the memory wire through a randomly chosen color dagger bead; then thread on a single seed bead.

4 Continue threading the beads on the wire, randomly choosing the color of the dagger bead as you work. To enhance the random look, occasionally place two dagger beads or two seed beads next to each other.

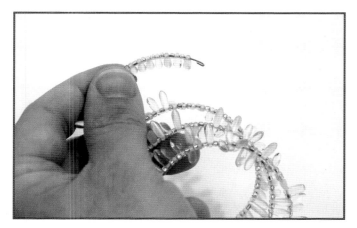

5 After stringing all the beads, cut off all but $3/8$ in. of the wire. Smooth the cut tip of the wire using emery cloth. Fold over a $1/8$-in. end of the exposed wire as in step 1, leaving a $1/8$-in.- wide space between the bent-in tip and the beads. This $1/8$-in. slack will allow the beads to swivel easily. Remove your protective goggles.

Subtle Color

A soft palette can be made more interesting by mixing beads with different textures. Here, water-clear glossy pink beads are intermingled with frosted pink beads and seed beads with mirrored interiors to create a romantic layered effect.

silver swirls capture luminous pearls

Floating Freshwater Pearls

This pretty bracelet is surprisingly easy to create. The main structure is made from a single length of silver wire that is bound together at key points and 'knit' together by the web of criss-crossing thin wire. The thin wire holds the bracelet together and captures the delicate freshwater pearls in champagne, taupe, and striking royal purple, giving an otherwise modern cuff a Victorian feel.

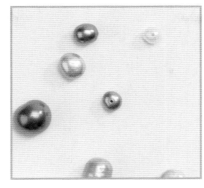

MATERIALS

- 30 assorted freshwater pearls:

    6 baroque or round, in pearl white, 8mm to 11mm,

    3 round, in pearl white, 4mm

    1 oblong, in gunmetal gray, 11mm x 7mm

    5 round, in taupe, 7mm

    4 smooth oval, in copper, 8mm to 10 mm,

    5 roundish, in gunmetal gray, 5mm

    2 roundish, in purple, 5mm

    1 lozenge, in coppery taupe, 13mm long x 7mm dia.

    3 round, in champagne, 8mm

- Sterling silver wire:
    16-gauge
    22-gauge
    24-gauge

TOOLS

- Wire cutters ■ Needle-nose pliers
- Emery cloth ■ Can or jar with stiff sides, 2½-in. dia. ■ Felt tip marker ■
- Denatured alcohol ■ Cotton swabs
- Adhesive tape

•••Making a Floating Pearl Bracelet

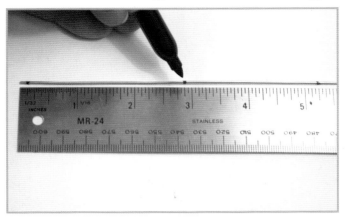

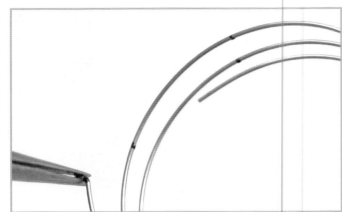

1 Cut a 28-in. length of 16-gauge wire. Using a ruler and a felt-tip pen, mark the wire at the following 10 intervals: $\frac{1}{8}$ in., 2 $\frac{7}{8}$ in., 5 $\frac{1}{4}$ in., 8 $\frac{3}{8}$ in., 10 in., 11 $\frac{1}{2}$ in., 13 $\frac{1}{8}$ in., 14 $\frac{1}{2}$ in., 19 in., and 21 $\frac{7}{8}$ in.

2 Wrap the entire wire length around the jar. Release the formed coil, and let it spring open. Smooth the wire ends using emery cloth. Bend the wire 90 degrees at the first mark ($\frac{1}{8}$ in.) with needle-nose pliers.

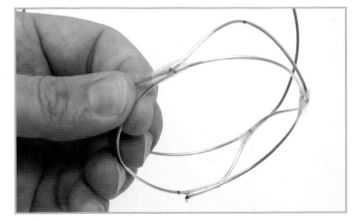

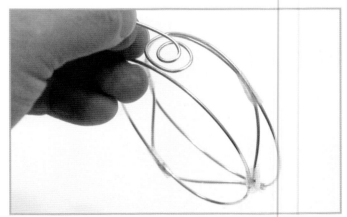

5 Continue to gradually shape the wire into gentle undulations, forming peaks and valleys at the next three marks. Roughly align the sixth and eighth marks with the marks on the closed ring, and tape these sections together.

6 Wind the free coil into a circle the same size as the closed circle and $\frac{3}{4}$-in. from it. Align the marks on the new circle with the undulating curves, and tape them together. Shape the remaining free wire into a spiral.

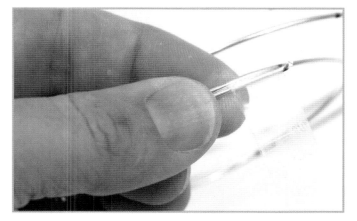

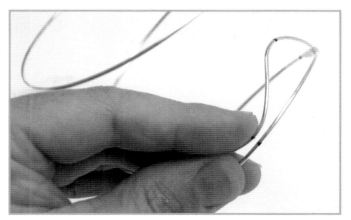

3 Align the first and fourth marks to form a 2½-in. diameter ring. Tape the wires together at this point to close the ring. Let the remaining coils of wire hang loose.

4 Using the tips of your forefinger and thumb, bend the coiled wire away from the closed ring. Apply even pressure for a smooth, gradual bend. Then bend the wire in the opposite direction, making a gradual curve that peaks at the fifth mark.

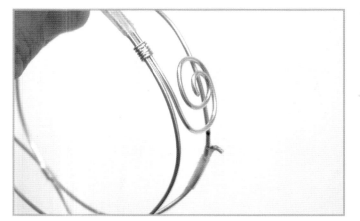

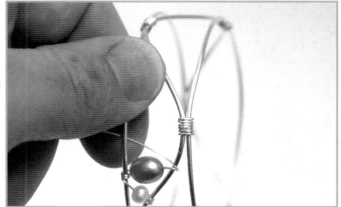

7 Remove the tape from one joint. Swab with alcohol to remove any marker residue. Cut a 2-in. piece of 22-gauge wire. Leaving a ¼-in. tail, wrap the wire tightly around the joint six times. Crimp down the tails. Repeat to secure each taped joint.

8 Cut a 7-in. piece of 24-gauge wire. Wind one end three times around the undulating wire, close to a joint. Crimp with pliers to secure. String on one pearl. Wind the wire around the outer ring several times to secure the pearl. Continue in this way to attach assorted pearls to the armature. Wind firmly, and crimp to end off. Use a new wire for each section.

shape and hue cascade together

Tumbling Crystals

A sophisticated palette can be achieved by limiting the range of hues in the chosen beads. Here, a very large smoky topaz with a tint of mossy green and citrines that range in color from pale orange to deep amber stand out among smaller background beads in champagne. Smokey quartz adds depth to the blond-to-amber color palette, making the look informal yet luxurious.

MATERIALS

- 58 quartz beads:

   1 irregular cut with facets, 27mm long x 22mm wide x12mm thick, in topaz with yellow-moss caste

   3 irregular cut, 23mm long x 18mm wide x 12mm thick, in citrine with pale to deep amber caste

   3 lozenge-shaped, 18mm long x 10mm wide x 7mm thick, in topaz with smokey caste

   1 briolette, pear-shaped, 13mm long x 13mm wide x 8mm thick, in smoke with yellow/green tint

   25 irregularly tumbled nuggets with crackle inclusions,13mm long x 6mm dia. in citrine with yellow/orange caste

   25 round faceted, 5mm dia. in pale yellow

- 3 citrines,18mm long x 14mm wide x 8mm thick, in pale to deep amber
- 44 freshwater pearls, 10mm long x 7mm dia. in champagne
- 1 set toggle clasp, rope design, 15mm dia.
- Nylon-coated tigertail
- 10 gold-plated round crimp beads
- 2 gold-plated split rings, 6mm dia.

TOOLS

- Wire cutters ■ Crimping tool
- Carpet needle

●●● Making a Tumbling Crystal Bracelet

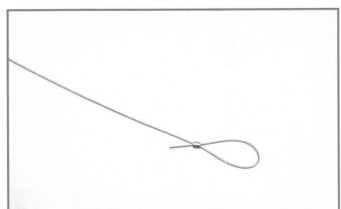

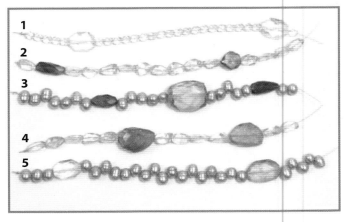

1 Cut five 9-in. lengths of tigertail using the cutters. Insert one end of a strand into a crimp bead. Fold over a $\frac{1}{2}$-in. length, and reinsert the tip back into the bead to form a $\frac{1}{8}$-in. diameter loop. Use the crimper tool to squash the bead to secure the wire loop. Repeat with the remaining lengths of tigertail.

2 Following the beading diagram pictured above, string the beads on Strand 1, leaving about 1 in. of tigertail unstrung. Gently set the strand aside on a flat work surface. Repeat to string the remaining strands, setting each down carefully when it is beaded.

5 Pry open one of the split rings using a carpet needle, and leave the needle inserted. Slide the end loop of one of the five strands into the gap of the split ring until the loop is entirely within the ring. Repeat the step to add the remaining strands and the bar section of the toggle clasp until they are trapped in the ring.

6 Lay the beaded strands on a flat surface. Lap the strands to "braid" them loosely together.

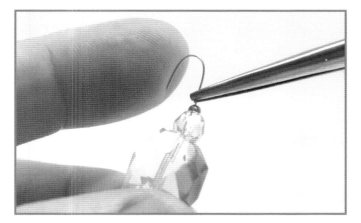

3 To finish Strand 1, thread a crimp bead on the end of the tigertail. Hold the strand vertically using needle-nose pliers. Turn the tail over and reinsert the tip back into the crimp bead to form a 1/8-in. diameter loop. Note: do not squash the crimp bead yet.

4 Pick up the strand and slide the crimp bead away from the last strung bead by about 1/16 in.*, and squash the crimp bead to secure the beads using the crimping tool. The finished strand will be about 8 in. long. Repeat steps 3–4 with the remaining strands.

*Note: this easement allows the strand of beads to flex around the wrist without binding.

7 Trap the bottom loops together at the ends of the beaded strands, slipping them, one at a time, into a split ring as in step 5.

8 To finish, slide on the hoop portion of the toggle clasp following the technique described in step 5.

faceted beads are like streams

Crystal Luster

The old-fashioned cut crystal beads in this bracelet have beautifully mirrored finishes that resemble marcasite. Surprising colors—scarab beetle green, nugget gold, and deep copper—appear when light reflects off the beads' surfaces. A matte gold medallion (that is actually a coat button) with a crystal accent adds an elegant finish to the bracelet.

of liquid metal

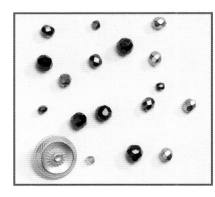

MATERIALS

- 253 Czech cut crystal beads in dark brown:

  25 round with aubergine luster, 7mm dia.

  25 round with dark green luster, 7mm. dia.

  25 oval with bronze luster, 6mm long x 5mm dia.

  100 oval with copper luster, 4mm long x 3mm dia.

  50 round with bronze luster, 3mm dia.

  28 round with bright gold luster, 3mm dia.

- 1 hot pink Swarovski crystal bead, 5mm dia.
- 1 card silk beading cord with needle attached, or 6½ feet
- 1 S-hook clasp, gold tone, 14mm in length
- 1 split jump ring, gold tone, 14mm dia., 10-gauge
- 1 button with center well, in matte gold, 2cm dia. x 4mm thick, with 4mm loop

TOOLS

- Sharp scissors ■ Beading glue
- Hook-nose pliers ■ Flat-nose pliers
- Small spring clamp ■ Carpet needle

••• Making a Crystal Luster Bracelet

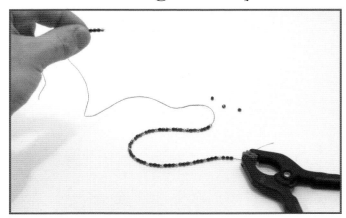

1   Unspool the silk cord from its card, and attach a spring clamp to 2 in. of the trailing end. Refer to the beading diagram to bead Strand 1 in a pattern of three 3mm round copper luster beads and one gold bead, using the needle that comes on the cord. Repeat the pattern until the strand measures 7 in.

2   Keeping the clamp attached at the opposite end, make a loose slip knot just above the end of the strung beads, capturing an open jump ring.

Lay the strand on a flat surface. Hold the tail of the knot and, with the other hand, use a carpet needle to slide the knot down to within $1/16$ in. of the last bead. Tie a square knot, using a drop of glue to secure it. Snip off the excess cord, using the scissors.

5   Insert one end of the open jump ring through the back loop of the button. Close the ring using the hook-nose pliers and the flat-nose pliers.

6   Decorate the button by adding a drop of glue to the open well in the center and placing the pink crystal bead inside. Turn the bead so the hole runs sideways and is somewhat hidden.

7   To ensure an easy fit when the bracelet is worn, pry open the top hook of the S-hook clasp as needed so it catches the jump ring.

3   Squeeze one of the hooks on the S-hook using your fingers. Carefully unclamp the beaded strand and tie the free end to this loop. Make a square knot, and use a dab of glue to secure it. Snip off the excess cord using scissors.

4   Repeat steps 1–2 to bead five more strands, attaching the strands, one by one, to the jump ring. After beading the strands, lap them in a loose braid, and attach the ends to the S-hook as in step 3. **Strand 2:** String a pattern of two oval 5mm beads with bronze luster interspersed by one round 3mm gold bead for 7 in. **Strands 3 and 4:** String fifty 3mm oval beads with copper luster onto each strand. **Strand 5:** String all round 7mm beads with aubergine luster. **Strand 6:** String all round 7mm beads with dark green luster.

diagram

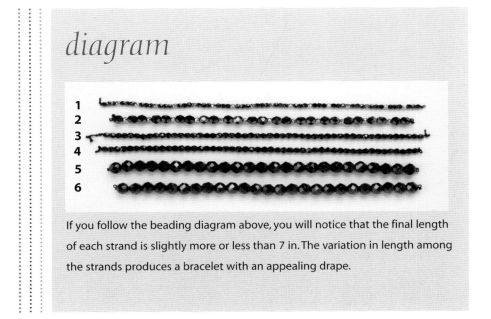

If you follow the beading diagram above, you will notice that the final length of each strand is slightly more or less than 7 in. The variation in length among the strands produces a bracelet with an appealing drape.

pretty blooms appear just-cut

Petaled Jewels

There is beauty in simplicity, as these beaded flowers testify. Made up

of beads called briolettes, the pear- or teardrop-shaped beads resemble real petals when strung together. The briolettes must be head-drilled (where the hole passes sideways across the narrow tip of the bead) to create the look. Use briolettes in mixed colors to create a choker with several multi-hued, five-petal blooms.

MATERIALS

For one orange flower:

- 5 quartz briolettes, pear-shaped, faceted, head-drilled, in orange, 18mm long x 13 mm wide x 5mm thick
- 1 pearl, oval, center-drilled, in pink, 8mm dia. X 6mm wide
- 1 seed pearl, in white, 2mm dia.
- 8" sterling silver wire, 20-gauge
- Transite

For one red flower (make 2):

- 5 quartz briolette beads, pear-shaped, faceted, head-drilled, in red, 16mm long x 12mm wide x 6mm thick
- 1 pearl, oval, center-drilled, in lime green, 8mm dia. X 6mm high
- 1 seed pearl, in white, 2mm dia.
- 8" sterling silver wire, 20-gauge,
- Transite
- ²⁄₃ yd. satin ribbon, in green, ⁵⁄₈" wide
- 1 set barrel clasp, in sterling silver, 9mm long x 4mm dia.
- 1 open jump ring, oval, sterling silver, 5mm long x 4mm wide

TOOLS

- Wire cutters ▪ Round-nose pliers
- Needle-nose pliers ▪ Thread cutters
- Emery cloth

••• Making a Petaled Jewels Necklace

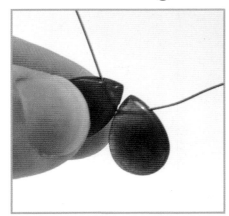

1 Cut an 8-in. length of wire. Thread it through one red bead, and slide the bead to the midpoint of the wire. Thread on a second red bead. Bend the wire so that the beads abut one another as shown.

2 Thread on the third and fourth red beads, positioning them at the sides of the first two beads. Add the remaining red bead to either side of the wire.

3 Twist the wire ends together at the base of the beads, using the needle-nose pliers. Tighten the twist so that the petals are drawn closely together.

Note: the beads are still floppy at this stage.

7 Cut one of the wire stems to a nub. Smooth the cut end with the emery cloth. Cut the other wire 2 in. beyond the twisted section. Roll the wire three times around the base of the round-nose pliers to make a loop.

8 Make a second red flower, if desired, following steps 1–7, as before.

9 Make an orange flower. Thread the ribbon through the wire loops on each flower. To add the clasp to the ribbon, see Classic Pendant Choker on page 53, steps 8–10.

4 Cut a 12-in. length of transite. Thread 3 in. through the center opening in the cluster of petals. Tie a square knot at the wire twist, leaving a slightly shorter-than-3-in. tail.

5 Bind all the beads in place by drawing the long tail of transite forward behind two beads and then lashing backward across one bead. Repeat to form a pentagonal pattern. Make two complete passes around the bead cluster—the petals will become nearly immobilized. Tie the end and the short tail in a square knot.

6 Turn the petal assembly over, and pull the longer tail of transite through the center hole to the front. Pass the transite through a pearl, a seed bead, and then back through the pearl. Pull the pearl close to the petals. Tie the transite tails in a square knot; trim to 1/8 in.; and tuck in the ends.

layout

The "flowers" are threaded on the ribbon, so they can be moved close together or far apart.

1 1/2"   The approximate diameter of each "flower."

2"   The distance from the center of one "flower" to the center of an adjascent "flower."

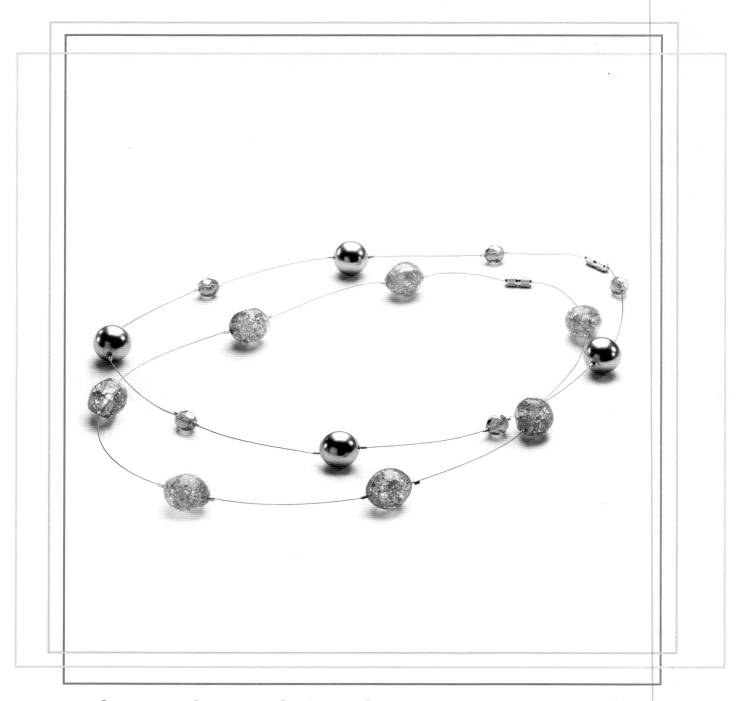

beads orbit dainty strands

Celestial Strands

These light-as-air strands of shimmering beads are actually

two necklaces that are carefully color-coordinated. The beads on both strands appear to float in delicate orbits. Crackled glass beads in peach, pink, and yellow-green are spaced evenly on the first strand. They are set off against copper-toned pearls and smaller amber beads on the second strand. Together, they look heavenly.

MATERIALS

For Strand 1:

- ■ 7 glass beads, oval, crackled, 13mm dia. X 15mm long:
    - 3 in yellow/green
    - 2 in pink
    - 2 in peach
- ■ 16 crimp tubes, silver tone, size 2 (1.3 dia. x 2mm long)

For Strand 2:

- ■ 5 glass beads, round, faceted, mirror finish, in amber, 8mm dia.
- ■ 4 pearls, in pale copper, 14mm dia.
- ■ 20 crimp tubes, silver tone, size 2 (1.3 dia. x 2mm long)

For both strands:

- ■ Braided wire, stainless steel, nylon-coated, 19 strands
- ■ 2 barrel clasps designed for hidden knots, aluminum, 1cm (4mm dia. x 10mm long)

TOOLS

- ■ Crimping tool ■ Wire cutters
- ■ Felt-tip marker, non-permanent
- ■ Ruler

Making a Celestial Strands Necklace

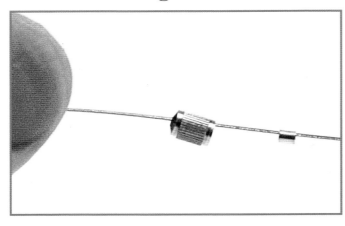

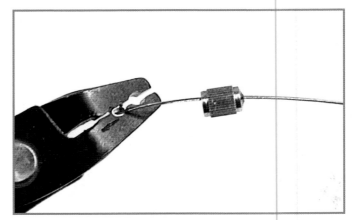

1 For Strand 1, cut a 20-in. length of wire. Thread one end of the wire through one-half of the barrel clasp and one crimp tube.

2 Fold over the end of the wire, and insert it back into the crimp tube. Secure the crimp tube using the crimping tool.

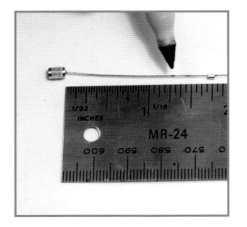

Stainless-Steel Wire

Nylon-coated stainless-steel braided wire is strong and flexible, yet soft to the touch and safe next to the skin because of its smooth protective coating. The surprisingly strong cable has a satin sheen that can be used to great decorative effect.

5 Measure 1¼ in. from the barrel clasp along the wire, using a ruler. Make a small mark on the wire to the right of that measurement with a felt-tip pen. Thread on a crimp tube to cover the dot, and secure it using the crimping tool.

6 Thread a yellow-green bead on the wire until it rests against the crimp tube. Thread on a second crimp tube so that it rests against the bead. Secure the crimp tube using the crimping tool.

Note: the crimp tubes will hold the bead in place.

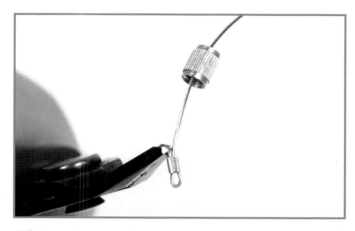

3 Snip off the end of the wire so that it is even with the crimp tube, using the wire cutters.

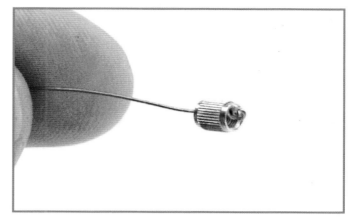

4 Slide the barrel clasp over the crimp tube, making certain it fits neatly inside.

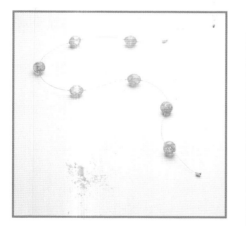

7 Follow the layout above to add the remaining six beads at 2-in. intervals. Repeat step 6 to secure each bead. Repeat step 1 to secure the other half of the barrel clasp at the end of the wire.

Crimp Tubes

The crimp tubes are a visible design feature on this necklace. Use crimp tubes that are suitably sized for the wire but thick enough to trap the beads. Choose beads with small holes so that the tubes don't slip into the bead, allowing them to slide around the strand.

8 For Strand 2, cut a 21-in. length of wire. Repeat steps 1–4 to attach one-half of the barrel clasp. Follow steps 5–8, and refer to the layout above to secure the beads and pearls at $1^5/_8$-in. intervals. Add the other half of a barrel clasp as before.

a sheer ribbon holds a
polished tablet

Classic Pendant Choker

This elegant choker achieves its sophisticated look through the bold use of a red, black, and silver palette. The color contrasts are heightened by the play among the surface textures: the polished gloss of the carnelian tablet, the matte gold of the findings, and the glowing luster of the accent pearl. All of the design elements of the pendant are enhanced by a satin-edged strand of sheer ribbon.

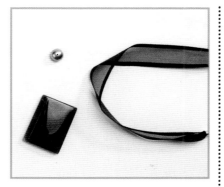

MATERIALS

- Carnelian stone, pillow-cut, center-drilled, in red, $1^{3}/_{8}$" high x 1" wide x $^{1}/_{8}$" thick
- 1 freshwater pearl, baroque, in champagne, 6mm dia.
- 1 seed bead, in gold, size 10/0
- 1 ball-head pin, sterling silver, 1" tail, 24-gauge, or thin enough to pass through the pearl
- 1 drop, cone-shaped, with top loop, in matte gold tone, $^{7}/_{8}$" high x $^{3}/_{16}$" dia.
- $2^{1}/_{2}$" sterling silver wire, 20-gauge
- $^{1}/_{3}$ yd. sheer ribbon with satin edge, in black, $^{5}/_{8}$" wide
- 1 barrel clasp, sterling silver, $^{1}/_{4}$" long x $^{1}/_{8}$" inner dia.
- 1 ring clasp, sterling silver, size small
- 1 cord connector, sterling silver

TOOLS

- Wire snips ■ Round-nose pliers
- Needle-nose pliers ■ 2 toothpicks
- Beading glue

••• Making a Classic Pendant Choker

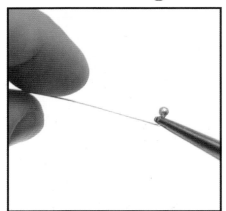

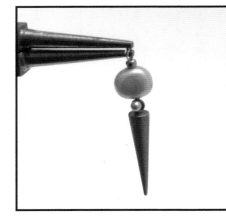

1 Grasp the head pin just behind the ball tip using the tip of the needle-nose pliers. Bend gently at a right angle to create a ¹/₁₆-in. space between the back of the ball head and the crook.

2 Thread the head pin through the top loop of the gold drop, the pearl, and the seed bead. Wind two full loops of the pin using the round-nose pliers so that the loops face sideways and the ball head faces forward. Snip off the excess pin.

3 Form an open loop ³/₄ in. from one end of the 2¹/₂-in. length of silver wire using the round-nose pliers, leaving a tail about ¹/₂ in. long. Thread on the beaded assembly.

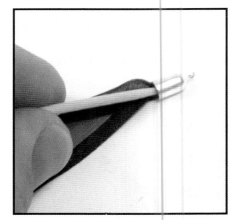

7 Fold one end of the ribbon length-wise, and thread it through the connector until the connector is at the midpoint of the ribbon.

8 Tie a slip knot at one end of the ribbon, pulling it tightly to form a hard ball that fits snugly into the tubular end of the barrel clasp. If needed, squeeze the knot using pliers until it is small enough. Trim off the excess ribbon so it is flush with the knot.

9 Apply a dot of beading glue to the ribbon knot. Seat the knot firmly in the barrel clasp, using the blunted tip of a toothpick. Repeat to add the other half of the barrel clasp to the other end of the ribbon.

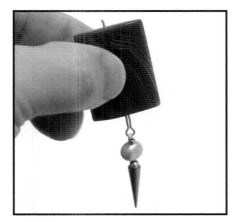

4 Insert both wire ends into the hole at the bottom of the tablet. Add a drop of beading glue to the tail before seating the beads all the way, facing the loop forward.

Note: this keeps the loops correctly oriented so that the pearl drop faces forward.

5 Bend the wire at the top of the tablet bead 45 deg. to the left. Roll a $1/8$-in.-diameter loop using round-nose pliers so that the loop opening is front to back. Wind the loop tightly against the bead so that the wire fits snugly and the bead cannot move up and down.

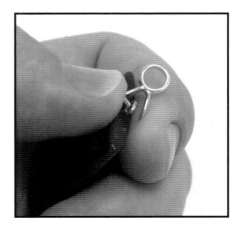

6 Install and crimp the silver connector to the top loop of the tablet bead as shown.

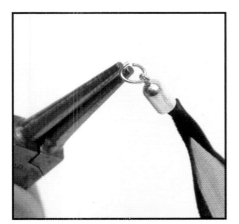

10 Use pliers to open a jump ring. Thread the end through the loop at the end of the clasp; close the ring. Repeat at the other end, adding a ring clasp.

design tip

Pillow-cut stones are prized for their unique silhouettes. Meant to be strung together to form cuff bracelets, some stones are beautiful enough to be featured as the centerpiece in one design. Look for stones that have distinct characteristics like a noticeable pattern or an interesting variegation of color. These qualities will distinguish the stone and make it worthy of "center stage."

flowers accent **a chain like dew**

Sweet Dewdrops

This disarmingly dainty necklace is accented by little crystal beads that,

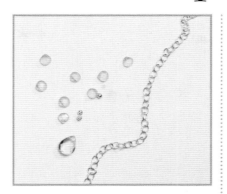

when clustered together, create the look of of little flowers. Even though each flower is made of beads in identical sizes, an optical illusion suggests beads in graduated sizes. The feather-weight necklace's foundation is a silver chain with a magnetic clasp, the ends of which seek each other out, making the necklace fumble-free when closing.

MATERIALS

- 17 quartz briolettes, pear-shaped:
  - 16 faceted, in rose, 6mm high x 6mm wide x 3mm thick
  - 1 in clear rose, 12mm high x 9mm wide x 5mm thick
- 7 spacer beads, sterling silver, hollow, 3mm dia.
- 24" chain, sterling silver, 2mm oval links
- 1 magnetic clasp, capsule-shaped, sterling silver, 12mm long x 4.5mm dia.
- 9 open jump rings, sterling silver, 2mm dia.
- 14" sterling silver wire, 26-gauge

TOOLS

- Round-nose pliers ▪ Needle-nose pliers ▪ Wire cutters

Making a Sweet Dewdrops Necklace

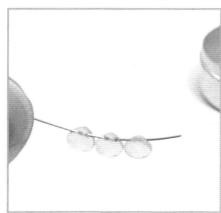

1 Cut the 14-in. length of silver wire into seven 2-in. segments using wire cutters. Thread one wire segment into three small briolettes, positioning the last one $\frac{1}{2}$ in. from the end of the wire.

2 Bend the wire so that the three beads press together edge to edge in a clover shape. Cross the long wire tail over the short tail.

3 Twist the tails together using your fingertips to form a loose three-bead cluster. The two petals closest to the twist should be $\frac{1}{16}$ in. apart.

Choosing a Clasp

The magnetic clasp is perfect for a feather-weight necklace. The ends of the clasp are self-centering, so they seek each other out. Choose one equal in diameter to a single link in the chain to keep the overall look delicate.

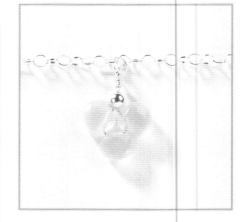

7 Repeat steps 1–6 to make the center cluster, using the large briolette as the center bead.

8 Thread each remaining 2-in. wire through a single briolette. Complete each briolette drop as you did the clusters.

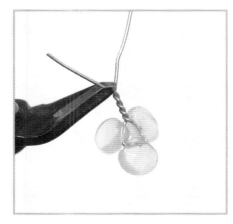

4 Rotate the bead cluster to form a twisted stem about $^3/_{16}$ in. long. Do not overtighten. Snip off the shorter wire.

Note:: the wire tails will be unequal in length.

5 Slide a round spacer bead onto the longer wire. Seat the spacer bead firmly against the bead cluster, concealing the twisted wire section.

Note: a single wire should emerge from the top of the spacer bead.

6 Create a $^1/_{16}$-in. loop in the single wire using round-nose pliers. Wind the tail around the stem until it presses against the silver bead. Snip off any excess, and tuck in the wire tip. Repeat steps 1–6 to make three more clusters.

9 Attach the center cluster to the center link in the chain with a jump ring, using needle-nose pliers. Attach the remaining four clusters to the chain, spacing them $1^3/_4$ in. apart. Attach the single drops $1^1/_2$ in. from the clusters on either side.

10 Attach one half of the clasp to each end of the chain by threading an open jump ring through the clasp loops on the the chain's last link, using the needle-nose pliers.

11 To add style, twist the necklace, as shown.

crystal tassels loop
through a swash of gold

Harvest Lariat

A lariat-style necklace is an amazingly versatile piece of jewelry. Its appeal lies in its nonconventional closure. Instead of a clasp, there is a loop at one end through which you thread the other end of the necklace. Usually, there is an eye-catching pendant, bead cluster, or tassel that provides a stylish focus for the strand that encircles the neck and cascades in sparkling color.

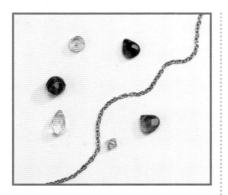

MATERIALS

- 30 faceted crystal beads

    24 assorted bi-cones, in amber, green, and smoke: 16, 3mm long, 3mm dia.; 8, 6-9mm long

    4 briolettes: 1 teardrop-shaped, head-drilled, in yellow, 13mm high x 7mm wide; 1 teardrop-shaped, center-drilled, in cranberry red, 7mm long x 5mm thick; 1 pear-shaped, center-drilled, in smoke, 13mm long x 13mm wide x 8mm thick; 1 pear-shaped, head-drilled, in brown, 11mm long x 9mm wide x 4mm thick

    2 rondelles, center-drilled, in clear amber, 8mm dia.

- 3 carnelian beads: 1 round, in orange/yellow, 10mm dia.; 2 rondelles, 9mm dia.
- 3 freshwater pearls, head-drilled, in champagne, 10mm long, 7mm dia.
- 2 hanks of seed beads, or 62", gold-plated, 1/2mm dia.
- Spool of stainless-steel beading cord, nylon-coated, thin, 19-strand
- 2 crimp tubes, gold tone, size 2
- 7 ball-head pins, gold-plated, 1 1/2" long, 26-gauge
- 7" wire, gold-plated, 24-gauge
- Gold chain, two 1/2" lengths, oval links, 3mm long x 2mm wide

TOOLS

- Wire cutters ■ Crimping tool
- Round-nose pliers ■ Needle-nose pliers ■ Emery cloth

Making a Harvest Lariat Necklace

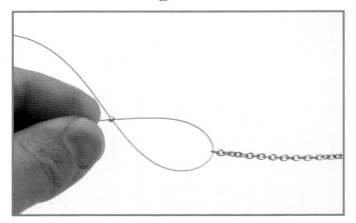

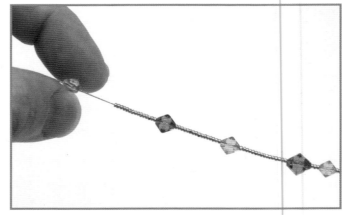

1 Cut a 60-in. length of nylon braid. Thread one end through a crimp tube, the end link of the gold chain, and back through the crimp tube. Slide the bead down to form a $^1/_{16}$-in.-dia. loop with a $^1/_2$-in. tail. Use the crimping tool to close the tube.

2 Thread the opposite end through an 8mm bead; slide it to the crimp bead and over the short tail. Thread on a gold seed bead, pale yellow rondelle, and bi-cone beads, interspersing them with $^5/_8$-in. spans of seed beads. After the last bicone bead, thread on 3 in. of seed beads and a smoke-color bead. Repeat this pattern, alternating the smoke, amber, and green beads, until all 14 in. of the nylon braid are used up, ending with an amber bead. Add another 3 in. of seed beads, followed by a green bi-cone bead, a crimp bead, and finally 6 in. of seed beads.

5 Thread the end of each pendant through one link in the gold chain. Form a loop to secure each pendant. Snip off the excess wire using wire cutters.

design tip

Braided wire is an ideal strand material for a lariat because it is somewhat springy and thus resistant to tangling —something to consider with a very long strand.

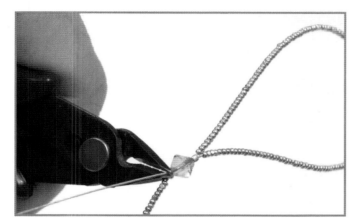

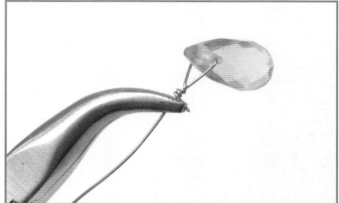

3 Insert the end of the braid into the other crimp tube and a green bi-cone bead. Pull it completely through to form a loop with no gaps. Use the crimping tool to secure the crimp tube. Snip off excess wire that sticks out past the green bead using wire cutters.

4 Refer to the beading layout to make 10 pendants. Use the gold seed beads as spacers. Use gold-plated wire instead of head pins to make the pendants that terminate in head-drilled briolettes.

layout

BEADED TASSELS

1: freshwater pearl **2: a.** crystal briolette, pear-shaped, smoke, 13mm long **b.** carnelian, rondelle, 9mm **3:** freshwater pearl, 10mm long **4: a.** crystal briolette, pear-shaped, brown, 11mm long **b.** crystal bi-cone amber, 6mm **c.** carnelian, rondelle, 9mm **5: a.** crystal bi-cone amber, 6mm **b.** crystal rondelle, clear amber, 8mm dia. **c.** crystal bi-cone, amber, 8mm **6:** freshwater peral, 10mm long **7: a.** crystal rondelle, clear amber, 8mm dia. **b.** carnelian 10mm dia. **8:** crystal briolette, tear drop-shaped, red, 7mm long **9:** crystal round, 10mm dia. **10:** crystal briolette, tear drop-shaped, in yellow, 13mm high

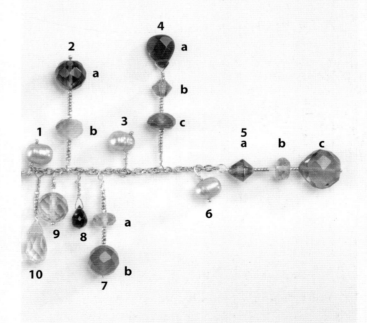

a floral crescent "whispers"

Winter Orchid

In this necklace, luster tells the design story. The satiny glow of rose quartz "petals" and pale green jade "leaves" are in concert with the delicate sheen of the polished silver branch and the iridescent freshwater pearls. The red garnet center of each orchid adds restrained drama, keeping the composition fresh and interesting.

rose and green hues

MATERIALS

- *9 quartz beads, heart-shaped, polished, center-drilled, in pale rose:*
    - *6 small: 11mm long x 11mm wide x 7mm thick*
    - *3 large: 15mm long x 15mm wide x 9mm thick*
- *2 jade beads, heart-shaped, satin finish, center-drilled, in soft mint green, 12mm long x 12mm wide x 4mm thick*
- *3 freshwater pearls, center-drilled, in white, 4mm to 6mm dia.*
- *3 garnets, round, in red, 4mm dia.*
- *36" sterling silver wire, 22-gauge*
- *40" sterling silver wire, 24-gauge*
- *18" sterling silver chain, 4mm x 5mm links*
- *2 open jump rings in sterling silver, 18-gauge wire, 4mm*
- *1 lobster-claw clasp, sterling silver, 12mm outer dia. x 5mm inner dia.*

TOOLS

- *Wire cutters* ■ *Needle-nose pliers*
- *Knitting needle or round stick ¹/₈" to ³/₁₆" dia.* ■ *Ruler* ■ *Emery cloth*

Making a Winter Orchid Necklace

1 Cut a 32-in. length of 22-gauge wire, and fold it in half. Slip a large heart-shaped bead, notched end first, onto one wire, and slide it to the bend. Stroke the wire down firmly along the back of the bead. Cross the wire tails at the pointed bottom of the heart, and twist twice with your fingers to trap the bead.

2 Bend one leg of the wire at a right angle ⁵/₈ in. from the twisted section. Thread another large heart bead onto the bent wire. Press the wire along the back of the new bead, as in step 1. Bring the back wire to the front and over the bead to form the twist. Make sure both beads are on the same plane.

3 Repeat step 2 to attach the third large heart bead to the other leg of wire.

7 Trap the bead as in step 1, and twist the wires 4 to 5 times to form a ¹/₈-in. stem.
Note: the base of the stem should be about ⁷/₈ in. from the base of the flower cluster. Splay the wires at the base of the stem.

8 Bend the wire ¹¹/₁₆ in. from the base of the stem. Repeat step 2 three times with the small heart beads to form a small flower cluster. Add a garnet bead to the center, and secure it, as in steps 4 and 5. The new flower cluster should be about ¹/₂ in. from the stem.

 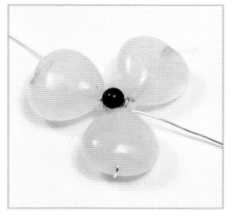 

4 Bring one of the wire legs to the front, pulling carefully but firmly. Thread on a red garnet bead, and seat it at the center of the three-petal cluster. Pass the wire down between the two opposite petals.

5 Loop the wire once again up and around one of the petals and then to the side to complete the flower cluster. Pull both wires in opposite directions to secure.
.

6 Bend one wire leg 1 in. from the base of the flower cluster. Thread a green jade bead, notched top first, onto the wire.

9 Repeat steps 6–8 to add a leaf bead and small flower cluster to the left of the large flower cluster.

10 Wind the wire once around the knitting needle 1¹⁄₂ in. from the left flower cluster. Twist the wires together, and pull tightly to shape a perfect circle. Remove the knitting needle. Repeat on the opposite side.

11   Wind each wire tail loosely around the connecting wire, gently nudging the beads aside as you work back toward the middle. Snip off any excess.

12   Place one end of the 24-gauge wire against the wire branch about ¹/₈ in. from the round loop. Wind once around the branch. Bend the short wire end up against the branch. Wind the longer end tightly around the branch until you reach the base of the loop. Bend down the short end, and crimp it with needle-nose pliers.

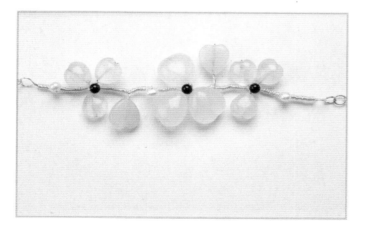

15   Bend the branch into an arc shape. Add small bends and crooks to simulate a natural tree branch.

Note: the finished bent branch measures 4 ¹/₄ in. long and about ³/₄ in. high.

16   Cut two pieces of silver chain, each 9 in. long. Join one end of each piece to an end of the branch using an oval jump ring. Attach a clasp and jump ring to the remaining two ends to close the necklace.

13 Wind the wire down the branch toward the flowers. Slip a freshwater pearl onto the wire, and trap it in the winds about 1/2 in. from the round loop. Adjust so the pearl faces forward.

14 Continue winding the entire length of the branch, placing the pearls as indicated in the diagram. At the other end, use the pliers to crimp the wind, trimming off the excess wire.

diagram

The configuration of petaled flowers and leaves is simple, providing enough room for each design element to be seen. The diagram here is a suggested layout. 4¼-in. length of "branch"

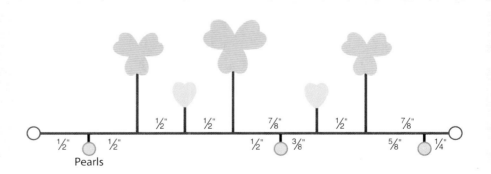

Pearls

red coral floats in a swirl of gold

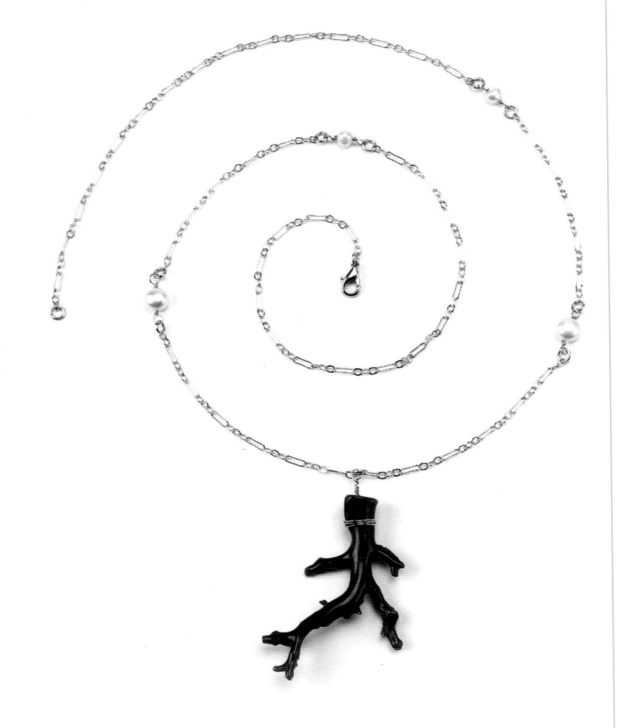

Coral Branch

Coral is a beautiful product of the sea. Its colors range from

pale shell pink to deep rich red, as well as to white and black. The orange-red color shown here is a classic shade. Genuine, naturally-colored coral can be expensive; however, dyed coral fragments that are reasonably priced are available. Look for coral with even coloring, a glossy polish, and stable branches for your necklace.

MATERIALS

- 1 piece of branch coral, 1 1/2" long-2" long x 3/16" thick at the thickest end
- 2 flat pearls, side-drilled, in white, 6mm dia. X 4mm thick
- 2 freshwater pearls, center-drilled, 4mm dia.
- 24" gold-filled chain, 2mm-dia. links
- 11" copper wire, gold-plated, 24-gauge
- 11 open jump rings, gold-filled, 4mm dia.
- 1 clasp set, gold-filled, 4mm dia.

TOOLS

- Wire cutters ▪ Jewelry glue
- Round-nose pliers ▪ Needle-nose pliers

••• Making a Coral Branch

1 Cut a 5-in. length of gold wire. Insert one end through the hole at the top of the coral, leaving a 1½-in. tail.

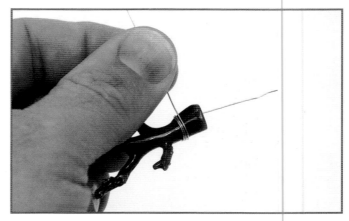

2 Wind the tail around the coral trunk several times, moving up from the hole and keeping the winds tightly together.

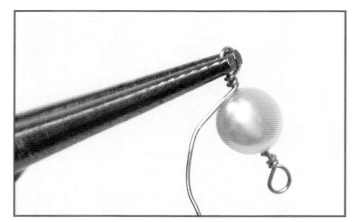

5 Cut four 2-in. lengths of gold wire. Thread one wire through a flat pearl, centering it on the wire. Make a tiny loop at each end, ⅛ in. from the pearl, using the very tip of the round-nose pliers. Repeat to make three more pearl links. See "Making a Double Loop" on page 134.

6 Lay the chain on a flat surface. Measure 2½ in. from the center link in both directions. At each location, snip out the nearest long oval link and the two round links adjacent to it. Join a large pearl link to each end of the chain using an open jump ring. Close each ring. Reattach the cut chains to the pearl links in the same way.

3 Tuck the remaining end of the wire into the side hole of the coral, and secure it with glue.

4 Form a loop with the short tail of wire, starting the bend about $\frac{1}{8}$ in. from the coral. Using the needle-nose pliers, thread one end of an open jump ring through the loop of the coral, and link it at the midpoint of the chain. Close the jump ring using hook-nose pliers.

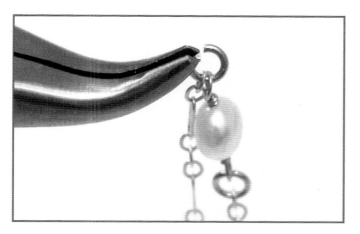

7 Measure $2\frac{1}{2}$ in. from the outside loop on each pearl link. Cut the chain, and remove links as in step 6. Rejoin the chain sections with the smaller pearl links, as in step 6. Attach a jump ring to one end of the chain and a jump ring and clasp to the other end.

Beaded Links

Here, the double-loop beads are comprised of white pearls. For a different look, consider using beads in red, such as natural carnelians. They will create an attractive continuum of monochromatic color.

delicate strands intertwine

Honey Gold Ensemble

Take one strand of pale gold beads in nugget style and another strand loaded with peridots and chunky crystals, and intertwine them with a gossamer sheer ribbon in gold to create a necklace of uncommon beauty. The interplay of subtle color is the backdrop for the bold contrasts in shape and size of the beaded decoration. It is this tension that creates a necklace with dynamic style.

MATERIALS

For the green bead strand:

- 10 ¹/₂" strand or 122 peridots, oval, faceted, in variegated green, 4mm dia. x 3mm thick
- 9 quartz crystal beads, faceted: 4 oblong, faceted, center-drilled, in pale yellow, 18mm long x 14mm wide x 8mm thick; 4 rondelles, in pale amber, 10mm dia. x 7mm thick; 1 teardrop-shaped, head-drilled, in pale yellow, 15mm dia. x 24mm long
- 2 crimp beads, size 1

For the ribbon strand:

- 4 quartz crystal beads, pillow-cut, faceted, in pale yellow/green, 12mm long x 9mm wide x 6mm thick
- ²/₃ yd. sheer ribbon with satin edge, in gold, ¹/₂" wide
- 2 jump rings, gold-plated, 8mm dia.

For the gold bead strand:

- 19 ¹/₂"-strand of seed beads, nugget-shaped, in gold, 12mm dia.
- 9 quartz crystal beads: 5 czech-style, barrel-shaped, in bright gold, 3mm dia. x 3mm long; 4 crystal beads, bi-cone, faceted, in amber, 3mm long x 3mm wide
- 2 crimp beads, size 1
- 1 clasp set, gold plated, 32mm overall length, 17mm outer dia.
- Transite

TOOLS

- Flexible beading needle ■ Thread cutters ■ Beading glue ■ 6 clamps
- Crimping tool

••• Making a Honey Gold Ensemble

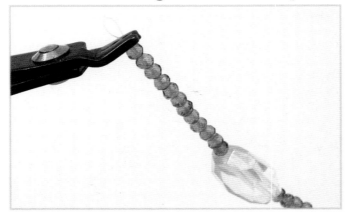

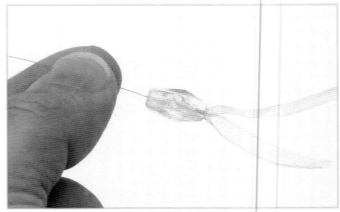

1 For the green strand, cut a 24-in. length of transite. Clamp one end. Thread the opposite end through 12 peridots, an oblong quartz in pale yellow, 12 peridots, a rondelle in pale amber, 12 peridots, an oblong quartz in pale yellow, 12 peridots, a rondelle in pale amber, and 12 peridots. Thread on the large teardrop-shaped bead. Clamp the end. Unclamp the opposite end, and thread on the beads in the same pattern but in reverse order. Attach a crimp bead to each end, using the crimping tool.

2 For the ribbon strand, insert a rolled end of the ribbon into a beading needle, and pull out 2 in. Push the needle through a pillow-cut quartz bead in pale yellow. Add the remaining quartz beads, spacing them at equal intervals along the ribbon. Position the first and last beads 3 3/4 in. from the ends of the ribbon.

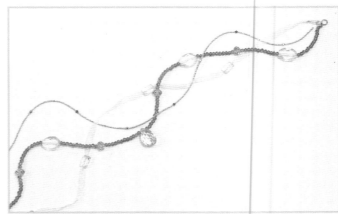

5 To assemble the necklace, thread the end of the open jump ring attached to the ribbon strand through the loops of the green strand and the gold strand, adding one part of the clasp. Close the ring, using needle-nose pliers and hook-nose pliers.

6 Lay the strands on a flat work surface, and loosely lap them into a soft braid.

Note: the tighter the braid, the shorter the necklace will be.

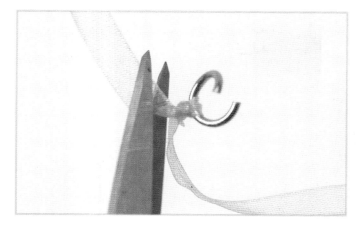

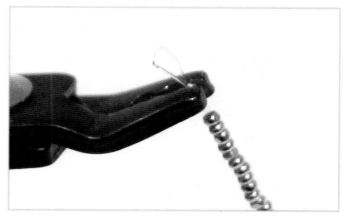

3 Tie one end of the ribbon to an open jump ring. Secure the knot with a drop of glue. Repeat at the opposite end. Neatly snip off the ribbon tails. Let the glue dry. Do not close the rings.

4 For the gold strand, cut a 24-in. length of transite. Clamp one end. Thread the opposite end through gold nugget seed beads to make a 1½-in. section. Add a Czech-style bead or a bi-cone crystal bead in amber. Continue the pattern, alternating seed beads with Czech beads or bi-cone crystal beads until a 1½-in. tail of transite remains. Attach a crimp bead, using the crimping tool. Repeat at the opposite end.

7 Repeat step 5 to join the strands at the opposite end; add the second part of the clasp, and close the jump ring, using hook-nose pliers and needle-nose pliers.

design tip

String only lightweight beads on the ribbon. Heavy beads will pull excessively on the fabric, causing it to sag unattractively. Also, make certain the chosen beads have large enough holes so the ribbon can pass through.

polished ebony tablets
form a scalloped circle

Burnished Ebony

Here, a classic and sophisticated red-and-black palette is boldly expressed in burnished tablets of ebony and glossy red carnelian stones. For this single-strand necklace, choose ebony tablets with a dense grain and good heft. Their color should be a deep brownish-black. For optimal contrast, use brightly polished carnelian stones in deep red so that they glow with inner fire.

MATERIALS

- 8 ebony beads, tapered tablets, drilled along their lengths, 2¹/₂" long x ³/₄" wide x ¹/₄" thick
- 7 red carnelian beads, 6mm dia.
- 16 spacer beads, gold filled, 3mm dia. x 2mm thick
- Elastic beading line, clear, 1mm dia.
- 1 barrel-shaped clasp, gold plated, magnetic, 5mm dia.
- 2 crimp beads, gold plated, size 2

TOOLS

- Thread scissors ■ Tweezers
- Crimping tool ■ Optional: beading needle

Making a Burnished Ebony Necklace

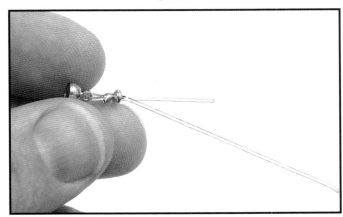

1 Cut a 25-in. length of elastic beading line. Thread on a crimp bead and one-half of the clasp by its loop. Insert the tip of the elastic line back through the crimp bead, and pull it to make a small loop with a 1-in. tail. Crimp the bead with a crimping tool to secure the assembly. Insert the opposite end of the line through a spacer bead, sliding it down to the crimp bead.

2 Thread the end of the line through the ebony bead. Slide the bead down to the spacer bead, and tuck in the tail.

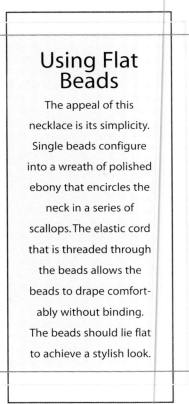

Using Flat Beads

The appeal of this necklace is its simplicity. Single beads configure into a wreath of polished ebony that encircles the neck in a series of scallops. The elastic cord that is threaded through the beads allows the beads to drape comfortably without binding. The beads should lie flat to achieve a stylish look.

5 Repeat step 1 on the free end of the beading line to attach the remaining part of the clasp. Tuck the tail of the beading line into the gold spacer bead and the ebony bead.

3 Thread on a gold spacer bead, one carnelian bead, and a second gold spacer bead.

4 Continue stringing all the beads in the same pattern, ending with a gold spacer bead.

design tip

Wooden beads are often drilled at larger diameters than other beads and require larger spacer beads as a result. These ebony beads have 2mm holes; at 3mm, the gold spacer beads are sufficient to cap the holes without slipping inside the bead.

Color Variation

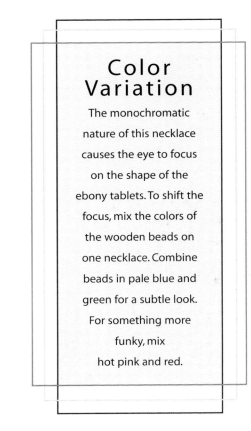

The monochromatic nature of this necklace causes the eye to focus on the shape of the ebony tablets. To shift the focus, mix the colors of the wooden beads on one necklace. Combine beads in pale blue and green for a subtle look. For something more funky, mix hot pink and red.

a trio of peridot strands resemble

Jeweled Wreath

Bead a trio of strands with chunky peridot chips, and attach

them to a bar-style clasp to separate the strands and show off their chunky silhouettes. Add hints of tomato red color by attaching highly polished carnelians on dainty loops. Finish by adding a large button in a lustrous matte gold, and you will have a necklace with individual high style.

graceful foliage

MATERIALS

- 2 strands of peridot, each 28" long, polished chips, in variegated green, approx. 5mm dia.
- 8 carnelian beads, in red:
  3 9mm dia.
  5 6mm dia.
- 8 gold head pins, 1½" long
- 1 button, gold vermeil, 30mm dia.
- 1 bar clasp set, three loops, 1³/₁₆" long bar
- 3" wire, gold-plated, 18-gauge
- Transite

TOOLS

- Wire cutters Round-nose pliers
- Hook-nose pliers Thread cutters
- Beading glue 3 clamps Beading needle

•••• Making a Jeweled Wreath Necklace

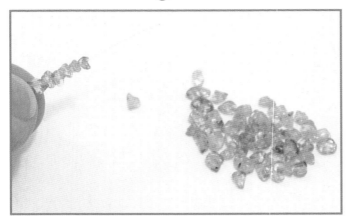

1 Cut a 20-in. length of transite. Clamp one end. Thread the other end on a beading needle. String on 18½ in. of peridot chips. Tie the end to the top loop of the bar clasp that has a dangling ball attached, using a square knot. Do not remove the clamp from the end of the transite.

2 Repeat step 1 to bead two more strands. Tie the strands to the remaining two loops on the bar clasp. Use scissors to snip off the excess transite at each loop. Secure each knot with a drop of glue, and let the glue dry.

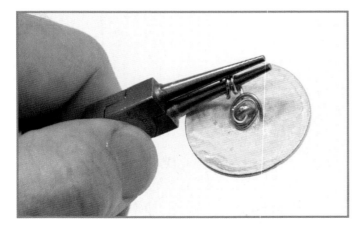

5 Bend one-half of the wire, and wind it around the loop on the button, using pliers. Use the round-nose pliers to wind the other half of the wire into a coil as shown.

6 Lay the midpoint of each peridot strand on the back of the button at the wire coil. Use pliers to bend the coiled wire over the strands to trap them.

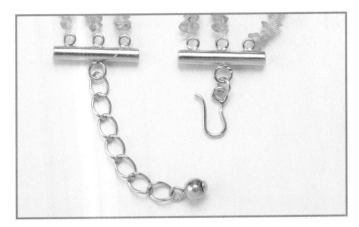

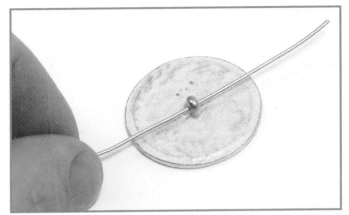

3 Remove the clamp at the end of the top strand strung in step 1, and tie the end to the middle loop on the hook side of the clasp, using a square knot. Repeat to tie the ends of the remaining beaded strands to the top and bottom loops on the clasp.

4 Thread the gold wire through the loop at the back of the button, sliding the button to the midpoint of the wire.

7 Thread a head pin through a carnelian bead. Bend the pin, and wrap it around the strand of peridot. Make a small loop, and snip off the excess pin. Add the remaining carnelian beads to the necklace in the same way, in positions as desired.

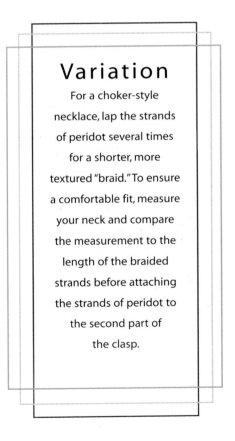

Variation

For a choker-style necklace, lap the strands of peridot several times for a shorter, more textured "braid." To ensure a comfortable fit, measure your neck and compare the measurement to the length of the braided strands before attaching the strands of peridot to the second part of the clasp.

watery clear crystals accented by

Crystal Pendant

The centerpiece of each of these earrings is a beautifully colored quartz bead that resembles a clear blue topaz offset by a small crown of faceted beads in rose, leaf, lime, and pale lemon colors. The smaller beads form a kind of berry cluster that moves freely when the earrings are worn due to the simple wire loops that join the pieces together.

MATERIALS

- 12 faceted quartz crystal beads:

    2 oval-shaped, in pale blue, 24mm high x 13mm wide x 7mm wide

    10 rondelles, in assorted colors, 10mm. dia., 4mm thick:

       2 rose

       2 pale rose

       2 lime green

       2 leaf green

       2 pale yellow
- 1 pair fishhook earrings, ball-tipped, in silver
- 12 ball-tipped headpins:

    2 2" long, 24-gauge

    10 1½" long, 18-gauge
- 2 small silver jump rings

TOOLS

- Wire snips ■ Round-nose pliers
- Needle-nose pliers ■ Flat-nose pliers

fruit-colored faceted beads   87

•••• Making Crystal Pendant Earrings

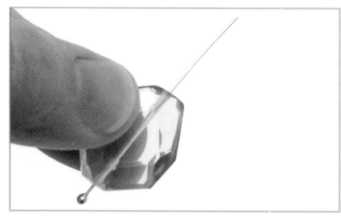

1 Insert the pointed end of a long head pin through the widest end of a blue quartz bead.

2 Grip the pin $3/16$ in. above the bead using the round-nose pliers. Rotate the pliers 45 deg. in one direction, and push the pin around the jaw of the pliers to form a loop.

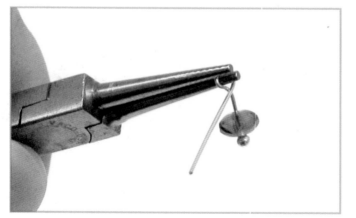

5 Insert the pointed end of a short head pin through one rondelle bead. Grip the pin $3/16$ in. above the bead, and make a loop following steps 2–4. Repeat to make loops on nine more rondelle beads.

6 Open a jump ring, and thread one end into the loops of six quartz crystal beads, following the order shown in the layout to the right.

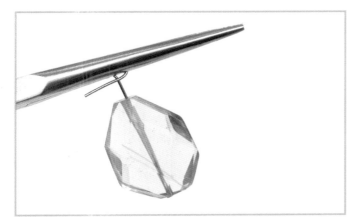

3 Remove the loop from the pliers. Use the widest part of the needle-nose pliers to firmly grip the face of the loop to flatten it.

Note: do not slide the pliers to avoid scratching the wire.

4 Wind the tail of pin around the stem of the loop to form a collar. Stop winding when the wire is about two turns away from the bead. Snip off the excess wire using wire cutters. Repeat to make a loop on the other blue quartz bead.

layout of quartz beads

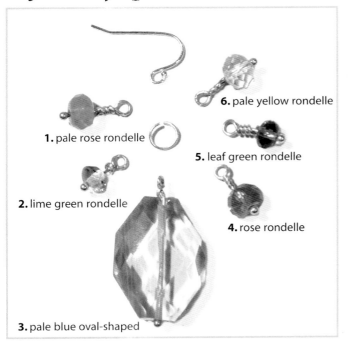

1. pale rose rondelle

2. lime green rondelle

3. pale blue oval-shaped

6. pale yellow rondelle

5. leaf green rondelle

4. rose rondelle

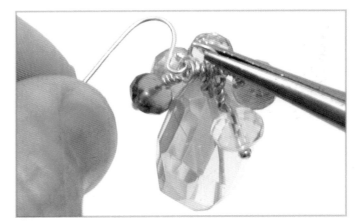

7 Thread the end of an open jump ring through the bottom loop on a fishhook earring. Close the ring using both sets of pliers. Repeat step 6 to make the second earring.

**crystals and gold chain
catch the light**

Chain Crystal Drop

The effect of liquid motion of these delicate earrings is pro-

duced by the lengths of extremely fine golden chain. Some strands are hung with stones; others are suspended at varying lengths; and together they create a cascade of lacy metal. Off-balance on the chain, the crystal beads seem to be moving even when they are still. When the earrings are worn, their swing throws off glints of light.

MATERIALS

- 10 crystal beads, teardrop-shaped, faceted, head-drilled:

  2 in lemon yellow, 13mm high x 7mm wide

  2 in smoke, 9mm high x 6mm wide

  2 in soft green, 10mm high x 6mm wide

  2 in bronze, 8mm high x 5mm wide

  2 in moss green, 7mm high x 5mm wide

- 22 open jump rings:

  2 gold-plated, 5mm dia., thick gauge

  20 gold-filled, 1mm dia., thin gauge

- 30" chain, gold-filled, 1mm links
- 2 fishhook earrings, ball-and-coil style, gold-plated
- 20" copper wire, gold-plated, 26-gauge

TOOLS

- Wire Cutters ■ Round-nose pliers
- Needle-nose pliers ■ Ruler

91

••• Making Chain Crystal Drop Earrings

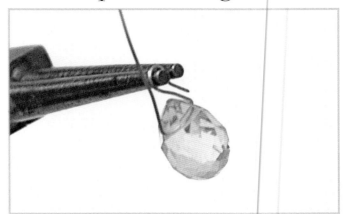

1 Cut a 2-in. length of 26-gauge gold-plated wire, and thread it through a bead so that $^3/_4$ in. of the wire extends beyond the hole. Bend both wires upward toward the tip of the bead.

2 Use round-nose pliers to form a loop directly above the tip of the bead. Push the wire against the side of the bead, and bend it into a crook shape.

Note: the loop of the "s" should be no larger than $^1/_8$ in. dia. on the smaller beads, and $^3/_{16}$ in. dia. on the largest bead. Trim off any excess wire, if necessary.

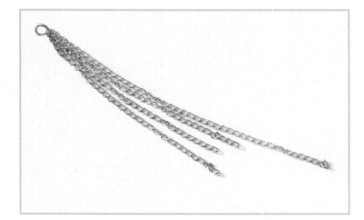

5 Cut the chain to the following lengths: five pieces, $1^1/_2$ in. long; two pieces, $1^1/_4$ in. long; two pieces, 2 in. long; and one piece, 1 in. long. Secure a small jump ring to one end of each chain. Close the jump rings with pliers. To make a chain cluster, secure the jump rings at the ends of one 2-in. chain, two $1^1/_2$-in. chains, and one $1^1/_4$-in. chain onto a small jump ring. Repeat to make a second cluster. Set them aside.

6 For the beaded strands, first secure a small jump ring to the loop of a lemon yellow teardrop and the end link of the reamining $1^1/_2$-in. chain. Use a small jump ring to secure a smoke teardrop $^1/_4$ in. above the lemon yellow teardrop. Then secure a small jump ring to the loop of a soft green teardrop and the end link of the 1-in. chain. To finish, use a small jump ring to secure a bronze teardrop $^3/_{16}$ in. above the soft green teardrop.

3 Hold the loop with needle-nose pliers, and bring the long wire around the back and over the front of the short wire's crook. Wind the wire down the side of the bead, covering the crook and the bead hole. Trim off the excess wire using wire cutters.

4 Use the needle-nose pliers to gently crimp the wires against the bead. Repeat for four more beads, each in a different color, and set them aside.

assembly layout

To assemble each earring, secure the chain clusters, the beaded chains, and the earring loop on the large jump ring using pliers. Repeat for the second earring.

a.   Lemon yellow teardrop and the smoke teardrop

b.   Soft green teardrop and the bronze teardrop

c.   Moss green teardrop

d.   Chain cluster

e.   Chain cluster

f.   Large jump ring

g.   Earring wire

delicate trefoils hold faceted jewels

Chandelier Drops

The irresistible appeal of faceted stones is show-cased here in a

quartet of "amethyst" beads suspended from a Celtic trefoil knot wound in silver wire. The sophisticated style of the earrings is based on the contrast between the polished luster of the silver wire and the sparkling clarity of the pillow-cut stones. Quartz stones come in a wide range of color, from pale lavender to the deepest purple.

MATERIALS

- 8 quartz beads, pillow-cut, faceted in smokey purple, 11mm long x 8mm wide x 5mm thick:
- 2 quartz beads, round, in rose, 12mm dia.
- 8 jade beads, round, in green, 4mm dia.
- 8 ball-head pins, sterling silver, 2" long, 18-gauge wire
- Sterling silver wire: 4" 22-gauge; 8" 18-gauge
- 2 earring hooks, sterling silver

TOOLS

- Round-nose pliers ▪ Hook-nose pliers
- Needle-nose pliers pliers ▪ Wire cutters ▪ Emery cloth

Making Chandelier Drop Earrings

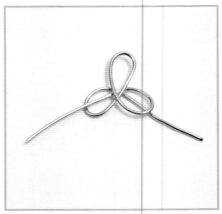

1 Cut a 4-in. length of 18-gauge wire. Use emery cloth to smooth the cut ends. Then bend the wire in half, and cross the left end over the right to form a long loop.

2 Bend the right wire end into a long loop, and bring it behind the loop made in step 1.

3 Bend the left wire end into a long loop, and bring it behind the loops made in steps 1 and 2.

7 Following the assembly diagram, secure a head pin loop to one of the trefoil loops by winding its end three times down the head pin. Trim off the excess wire. Close the head pin. Repeat for the remaining head pins.

8 Cut a 2-in. length of 22-gauge wire. Make a $1/8$-in.-dia. loop at one end, and secure it to the top loop of the trefoil. Thread the round quartz bead on the wire.

9 Make a $3/16$-in.-dia. loop in the other end of the wire. Wind the wire two times down the wire.

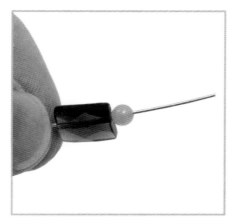

4 Bend the left wire end into a small loop, and bring it behind the loop made in step 3. Bend the right wire end into a small loop, and bring it in front of the loop made in step 2.

5 Thread a head pin through a pillow-cut quartz bead and a jade bead.

6 Use round-nose pliers to make a crook in the wire ⅛ in. above the jade bead, bending the wire around the nose of the pliers to make a ⅛-in.-dia. loop. Repeat for all head pins.

10 Use needle-nose pliers to open the loop in an earring loop. Slip the top loop of the round quartz bead onto the earring loop. Use the pliers to close the loop.

layouts

MAKING THE TREFOIL

Use the photo at right to guide the bending of the wire to make your trefoil.

ASSEMBLING THE EARRING

Use the photograph at right to guide you when assembling the parts of each earring.

a water-clear jewel accents
a golden disk

Gilt Spiral

The elegant symmetry of these earrings is achieved by balancing the geometry of simple shapes—a teardrop, an oval, a circle, and a hook—with interesting textures. Central to the design is a spiral of gold seed beads. Made by winding a strand of beads into a disk, the spiral adds glow and luster to the earrings. At the bottom of the spiral disk is a pendant of faceted aquamarine crystal.

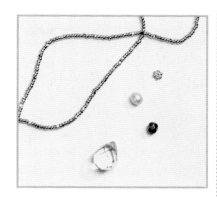

MATERIALS

- 12" glass seed beads, gold-plated, 11/0
- 2 seed pearls, in white, 4mm dia.
- 2 crystal beads, barrel-shaped, center-drilled, in copper luster over dark bronze, 4mm dia. x 4mm high
- 2 briolettes, teardrop-shaped, faceted, head-drilled, in pale aquamarine, 8mm dia. x 11mm high
- 2 daisy spacers, ball-filigree edged, matte gold, 3mm dia. x 1mm thick
- 23" copper wire, gold-plated, 24-gauge
- Transite, clear
- 4 crimp beads, gold-plated, size 1
- 2 fishhook earrings, ball-and-coil, gold-plated

TOOLS

- Wire cutters ■ Needle-nose pliers
- Crimping tool ■ Transparent adhesive tape ■ Round-nose pliers
- Sewing needle with eye large enough for transite to go through

Making Gilt Spiral Earrings

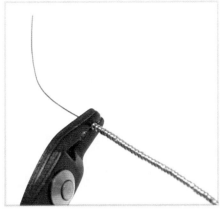

1 Cut an 8-in. length of wire. Use pliers to form a 1/16-in. loop at one end. Thread on a crimp bead over the loop, and secure it using a crimping tool.

2 Thread 6 in. of seed beads onto the wire. Slip on a crimp bead next to the last seed bead, and crimp it in place, leaving a 2-in. wire tail.

3 Bend the bead end of the wire into a tight loop using the tips of the needle-nose pliers. Wind the beaded wire into a spiral around this loop.

7 Thread the wire end through a pearl, and make a loop. (Refer to "Making a Wire Loop," on page 130.) Trim off the excess wire. Open the loop in an earring wire, and attach it to the loop above the pearl. Close the earring loop.

8 Cut a 2-in. length of wire. Thread the wire through the teardrop bead so that 3/4 in. extends beyond the hole. Make a loop at the top of the bead. (Refer to "Making a Wrapped Loop," on page 132.)

9 Cut a 1 1/2-in. length of wire. Make a loop in one end, and secure it to the teardrop bead. Thread the other end of the wire through a spacer bead and a bronze bead.

4 After a few turns, release the pliers and form the spiral by hand. Make the spiral as tight as possible. When finished, use a strip of tape to temporarily hold it in place.

5 Use the needle-nose pliers to bend the wire end of the spiral at a 90-deg. angle.

6 Cut a 6-in. length of transite, and tie it to the base of the wire end. Thread the other end of transite onto a needle. Stitch across the spiral, through the tape, securing each row to the next one. Tie off the transite, and snip off the excess. Remove the tape.

10 Thread the wire through the bottom row of the spiral, and make a loop. Wrap the end three to four times down the wire, and trim off the excess wire.

assembly layout

The parts of the earring are connected using loops.

a. Earring hook

b. Pearl

c. Spiral disk

d. Crystal bead with copper luster

e. Crystal bead with wrapped loop

Note: suspending a bead pendant puts stress on the disk. Stitch the spiral rounds together securely to prevent the disk from sagging.

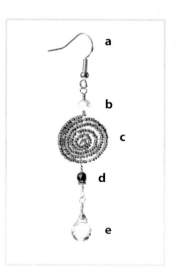

a faceted teardrop accents a

Grape Cluster Drops

The appeal of these earrings is the neat little bundles of pearls

that form the central design element of each pretty earring. The pearls stand out in elegant contrast against the simple wraps of silver wire that bind them together. Crystal clear teardrop beads swing like pendulums when the earrings are worn.

quartet of pearls

MATERIALS

- 8 pearls, oval, center-drilled, 7mm high x 9mm dia., in assorted colors:
  - 2 pink
  - 2 pale green
  - 2 olive green
  - 2 champagne
- 2 quartz beads, teardrop-shaped, faceted, head-drilled, in clear, 13mm high x 7mm wide
- 27" wire, sterling silver, 24-gauge
- 2 earring hooks, ball-and-coil, sterling silver

TOOLS

- Wire cutters ■ Needle-nose pliers
- Round-nose pliers ■ Hook-nose pliers

••• Making Grape Cluster Drop Earrings

1 Cut a 12-in. length of wire. Thread the wire through four pearls, leaving a 1½-in. tail extending from the last pearl. Cross the short wire tail over the long wire tail to form the pearls into a rough square.

2 Use the tips of needle-nose pliers to twist the wires together three times.

5 Insert the long wire end into the center of the pearls, and exit at the side opposite the short wire end.

6 Use the round-nose pliers to make loops in the long and short wire tails, trimming off the excess wire as needed. (Refer to "Making a Wire Loop," on page 130.)

3 Wrap the long wire between the pairs of pearls as shown.

4 Insert the long wire through the center of the pearls to the back as shown. Then wrap the wire in the other direction four times between the pairs of pearls.

7 Thread a 1½-in. length of silver wire through a teardrop bead, leaving a ¾-in. tail. Bend the wires up, and twist them three times. Thread the wire tail through the loop in the pearl cluster. Bend and wrap the wire to form a loop.

8 Open the loop in one earring wire, and thread on the loop of the pearl cluster. Close the earring loop. Repeat steps 1–8 to make the second earring.

crystal baubles look chic

Threaded Crystal

Traditionally styled rings have stones that are mounted in settings. However, stones with center-drilled holes, like those used for stringing a necklace, can be threaded onto wires and wound into rings. The appeal of using a winding technique to make a ring is that you can use beautiful beads in any color and shape to custom-make a ring that suits your personal taste and fits your finger perfectly.

MATERIALS

For ring with green center bead:

■ *1 glass bead, teardrop-shaped, faceted, center-drilled, in iridescent-clear green, 25mm long x 12.5mm wide x 7.5mm thick*

■ *2 aventurine crystals, round, in red, 5mm dia.*

■ *13" wire, sterling silver, 16-gauge*

For ring with pink center bead:

■ *1 glass bead, teardrop-shaped, faceted, center-drilled, in iridescent-clear pink, 23mm long x 14mm wide x 11mm thick*

■ *2 crystal rondelle beads, faceted, in pale lime green, 6mm dia. x 4mm thick*

■ *13" wire, sterling silver, 16-gauge*

TOOLS

■ *Dowel, 6" long x ⅝" dia.* ■ *Wire cutters* ■ *Needle-nose pliers* ■ *Emery cloth, 400 grit*

••• Making a Threaded Crystal Ring

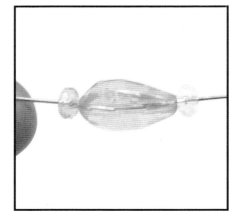

1 Thread the wire end through a small bead, the large bead, and the remaining small bead. Cluster them in the center of the wire.

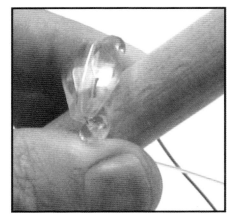

2 Position the bead cluster on one side of the dowel, and bend the wires to the other side as shown.

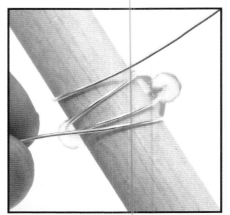

3 Holding the cluster with your thumb, wrap one wire end twice around the dowel, ending where you began. Repeat for the second wire end.

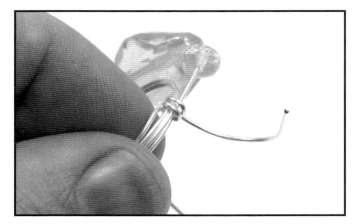

7 Wind the wire around the band of the ring three to four times, winding toward the bead. Repeat steps 6 and 7 for the other side of the ring.

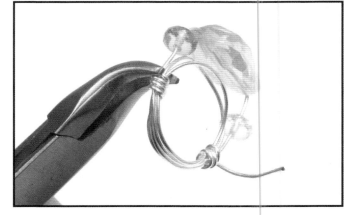

8 Cut the wire tails close to the band of the ring, and smooth the ends with emery cloth. Use needle-nose pliers to crimp the windings.

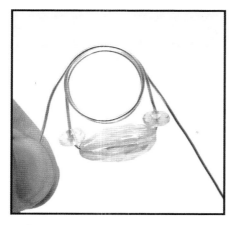 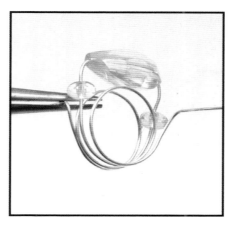 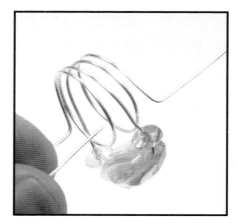

4 Remove the ring from the dowel, and test-fit it to your finger.

Note: tighten or loosen the wire loops to adjust the inside diameter of the ring.

5 Once the ring is adjusted, bend the wire tails at a 90-deg. angle away from the ring, just below each side bead.

6 Form one wire tail into a curve, and thread it through the ring.

design tip

Any wire can be used to make this ring, but sterling silver is ideal because it is easily manipulated yet holds its shape. Silver-plated wire is not as pliable, and the plating wears off readily

crystalline petals shimmer

Crystal Daisy

Tie a handful of dagger beads together, and add a plump faceted crystal to make a pretty "spring flower" for a ring. Half-hitches secure each petal-shaped bead to a foundation ring that is then attached to a quartz ring. For a striking bloom on your finger, choose dagger beads in luscious reds, oranges, or yellows.

in delicate **color**

MATERIALS

For the pink daisy ring:

- 18 quartz dagger beads, in hot pink, 10mm long
- 1 quartz bead, round, faceted, in clear green, 12mm dia.
- Transite, clear
- 6" gold wire, 24-gauge
- 2" silver wire, 20-gauge
- 1 split ring, chrome steel, 8mm dia.
- 1 quartz base ring, in translucent pink, sized to fit

For white daisy ring:

- 18 dagger beads, in iridescent pink, 10mm long
- 1 quartz crystal bead, round, faceted, in translucent orange, 10mm dia.
- Transite, clear
- 2" silver wire, 20-gauge
- 6" silver wire, 24 gauge
- 1 split ring, chrome steel, $^3/_8$" dia.
- 1 quartz base ring, in translucent yellow, sized to fit

TOOLS

- Thread scissors ■ Optional: large sewing needle

Note: the directions detail the making of the pink daisy ring; however, they can be followed to make the white daisy ring. Refer to the materials list above for the right items.

••• Making a Crystal Daisy Ring

1 To make the large pink daisy ring, cut a 16-in. length of transite. Use a double knot to tie one end of the transite to the chrome ring.

Note: pink transite is used to show the step more clearly.

2 Thread the other end of the transite into one dagger bead, sliding the bead so that it touches the ring. Secure the bead with a half hitch by inserting the transite end down through the center of the ring and up through the loop just formed. Pull the strand firmly to take up the slack, and keep your thumb securely on that bead while proceeding to the next bead.

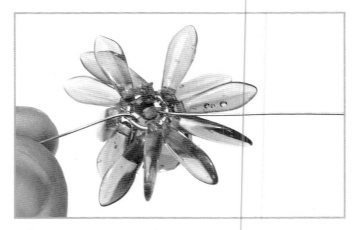

5 Thread the wire ends through the top center of the petal ring assembly. Pull the wires apart to seat the bead firmly against the petal ring.

6 Wrap the wires around opposite sides of the petal ring. Trim the wire ends to $1/16$ in., and tuck them under the petals to conceal them.

3 Repeat step 2 to secure nine dagger beads to make a row of "petals" around the ring. Secure the row with a knot. Use the same method to tie on eight more dagger beads, tying them between the beads in the first row. Set the petal ring assembly aside.

4 Thread the end of the 6-in. length of gold wire through the round green bead, sliding it to the center of the wire. Bend the wires down and flush against the sides of the bead.

7 Wrap the 2-in. length of wire around the base ring and the petal ring, binding them together as shown. Trim the wire end to 1/16 in., and tuck it under the petal ring.

8 Apply small dots of beading glue to the base of the dagger beads to stabilize them, and to the wire windings located under the beads.

BEADING BASICS

ALL THE TOOLS, MATERIALS, AND TECHNIQUES YOU'LL NEED

Basic Tools

The goal of this section is to help you set up a basic kit of beading essentials so that you can make every piece of jewelry in "The Collection," including those of your own design. You will probably want to add more enhancements to your kit as your interest in beading grows. In all cases, however, the number of essential tools needed to begin is surprisingly small. Although not shown, some household items like cotton swabs and tape are also needed.

●●● Tools

Round-Nose Pliers

Essential for making smooth and round loops in wire, these pliers can be identified by their conical, tapered jaws.

Needle-Nose Pliers

Easily found in hardware stores, needle-nose pliers are readily available from jewelry suppliers and craft stores specializing in beading. They come in a wide range of sizes. Look for ones that fit comfortably in your hand, with tips that come to a narrow taper. Spring-loaded handles that stay open are very useful for beading as they allow for easier handling. The inside surface of the jaws should be smooth rather than serrated so that the pliers don't leave impressions on findings and wire. Some pliers will have a built-in wire cutter that is fine for emergency use, but these cutters generally produce unacceptably jagged cut ends in wire.

Flat-nose Pliers

The jaws of this style plier are smooth and flat, making them suited to grabbing small jewelry-making items that are within easy reach. The tips of these pliers, however, are not tapered, making them clumsy when you need access to narrow recessed spaces.

GETTING STARTED

Here is an illustrated glossary of the essential tools you will need to make glamorous beaded jewelry. Some tools are indispensable to beading whether you are a beginner or veteran beader. Some tools are nice to have, making certain beading techniques slightly easier to do. Inexpensive tools may be adequate for occasional use, but when you begin to bead more seriously, you may decide to upgrade your tools to ones that are of better quality. Consider the list here before you begin.

Wire Cutters and Snips

Similar in appearance to a pair of pliers, wire cutters are actually pincers designed to cut wire with ease. If you have trouble cutting with them, try a pair with larger handles that will give you better leverage.

Spring Clamps

Clothes pins and alligator and binder clips can be used to keep beads from slipping off the end of strand material, but a spring clamp that has soft plastic pads is better for gripping beads without damaging them. Small 2 to 3-in. models work well.

Crimping Tool

Designed for squashing crimp beads and crimp tubes that secure strand material, this tool is easily found in craft stores. Designed with two indentations on its jaws, one flattens the crimp bead and the other folds it over tightly to produce a neat "stop" that keeps beads from sliding off the strand.

Thread-Cutting Scissors

A pair of sharp scissors in this style is much better than regular household scissors. Designed for making clean cuts in fiber strands, their perfectly aligned, fine steel blades make a much neater cut without causing fraying. Their characteristically sharp tip is also handy when trimming down a cord neatly to a nub.

••• Tools

Dowel Stick

Round sticks are useful when bending or shaping wire. Whether a dowel or a toothpick, round sticks provide a uniform diameter for making loops and rings and do not yield when the jewelry-making wire is wound around them.

Glue

Adhesive shouldn't be used as the primary means of assembling a beading project, but it can add extra security to tied knots in silk cord or transite line. It can also be used to attach bead caps to the end of memory wire. "Instant" glue and beading glue provide strong, permanent bonds.

Tweezers

Tweezers make it easy to pick up tiny beads and to hold and twist loops in fine wire. Tweezers are available in different styles with ends that are straight, angled, or tapered.

Wooden Beads

Round beads made of wood are excellent spacer beads, especially when you are constructing a piece of jewelry comprising two parts that need to be kept apart. Wooden beads come in various diameters, so you can always find the size that you need. Softer than most beading materials, the wood will not scratch or mar surfaces.

Beading Needle

With thicker or stiffer strand material, a needle is not essential. But with thinner and harder-to-see material, such as transite, a beading needle can be very helpful. Essentially a doubled-over and twisted piece of very thin wire, a beading "needle" can be made easily or can be purchased in inexpensive packs.

Emery File

Made to smooth down metal, an emery file is suited to smoothing metal in recessed areas, particularly handmade jump rings and squashed crimp beads. The emery material is also available in cloth. To use it to smooth the ends of wire, lay the cloth on a flat surface. Drag the rough wire end over the cloth, rotating the wire until a smooth end is produced.

Crochet Hook

Borrowed from needlework, the crochet hook is a handy tool that makes it easy to pull a cord through a knot or to get hold of a wire loop that's hard to reach.

Clamps

Small plastic clamps are easy to find in hardware stores. They are lightweight and suited to anchoring fine wire or other strand material. They are easy to manipulate, as they are designed with a spring-loaded joint.

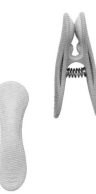

Containers

Keeping beads organized is very helpful. Use lidded containers to keep beads together, or at the very least, use resealable clear storage bags (like sandwich bags in smaller sizes) to help group similar beads together.

OTHER OPTIONS FOR YOUR BEADING KIT

Stackable Vials As you become more serious about beading and you accumulate a collection of beads, consider upgrading your containers to stackable vials. These come in various sizes and are made in a variety of materials, such as clear plastic, glass, and aluminum with glass tops. Containers made in transparent materials allow you to scan your collection quickly for the desired beads.

Molded Beading Tray Beads will roll if placed on a flat table. To avoid this, invest in a flocked beading tray that prevents beads from bouncing. The trays are designed with concentric, arc-shaped grooves, handy for composing the design of your strands before you start beading. The trays can be set aside in the middle of the project and set out again when you are ready to continue to bead.

Painter's Palette Available at art supply stores, a painter's palette has shallow wells in which you can distribute your beads. There are heavier palettes made of ceramic that are more stable than the palettes made of pressed metal although they are more expensive. Another option is to use disposable plastic palettes or cans with snap-on lids.

Needle-Threader A commonplace item, the needle-threader has a fine wire loop on the end of a plastic handle that opens up when it passes through the eye of the needle. Thread is inserted into the loop, and the loop is withdrawn from the eye of the needle, taking the thread with it.

Bench Clamp An inexpensive clamp that attaches to the edge of a table can be very handy as a "third hand" when you are carrying out a technique that requires both hands.

Basic Materials

••• Beads

This illustrated glossary of bead styles is designed to help you identify the kinds of beads used in the making of the pieces of jewelry in "The Collection." While there is an infinite number of beads available to you, these few represent the basic categories of bead styles. They are grouped by their dominant characteristics such as shape or surface finish. Some beads fall naturally into two different groups.

Round

Round beads come in the classic ball shape. Their size is identified by diameter (dia.) which can range from 2mm (tiny) to 15mm (large). The holes on round beads are drilled through their centers. They are available in an infinite variety of materials, colors, opacities, and surface finishes.

Oblong and Oval

Oblong and oval beads are usually drilled through their long axis, although some are drilled through one end so they can be offset in a design. They are measured by length and by thickness. Dagger beads are typical beads in this style group.

Rondelle

Rondelle beads are round beads that are flattened along the drilled axis, like a summer squash. They can be faceted or smooth, and they are made in materials from plastic to crystal.

Nugget

Nugget beads refer to any irregularly cut stones. A tumbled nugget is treated to agitation that polishes its surfaces. Nuggets have an organic look, like they have been mined from the earth.

Faceted

Faceted beads have flat cuts across their surface that reflect light, making them sparkle. They may be uniformly geometric in shape, or they may have irregular shapes with irregularly-sized facets. Crystals fit into this group.

Briolettes

Briolettes are pear-shaped or teardrop-shaped beads that can be polished or faceted. Slightly plump in profile, they have head-drilled holes across their tips so they look like drops when they are strung on a strand.

Teardrops

A teardrop bead fits in the briolette group. Its name describes its shape. It can be distinguished from the pear-shaped briolette by its elongated silhouette. Made in plastic, glass, and precious stone, these beads are usually used as accent beads or pendants.

Bi-cone

Bi-cone means "two cones," which accurately describes the shape of these beads. Crystal bi-cones come in either a faceted or polished finish. Their holes are drilled along their axis.

Chips

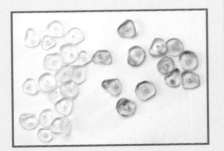

Chips refer to any fragments of glass, stone, or other material that are irregular in size, often the result of breaking. Often polished until smooth, they have center-drilled holes.

Quartz

Quartz is a versatile mineral that is naturally snowy white, gray, or rose in color. Quartz is dyed to change its color and cut with facets to simulate semiprecious stones.

Pearls

Pearls are not just the classic round pearly-white, expensive gems they once were. Improved dyeing techniques now produce pearls in fun colors. Pearl varieties include freshwater pearls that are cultivated, producing interesting shapes. Silk thread is recommended for stringing pearls.

Seed Beads

Seed beads, also known as rocaille beads, come in an infinite variety of colors, finishes, and materials. They are commonly sold on hanks that comprise several beaded strands. Seed beads are measured by number— the higher the number, the smaller the bead.

Lustrous

Lustrous beads have a metallic sheen on their surface that makes them appear to glow. Made in stone, metal, glass, and quartz, lustrous stones complement beads that are faceted and sheer, like bi-cone crystals. Fire-polished beads are noted for their luster.

Crackled

Crackled glass beads have natural or manufactured fissures or striations in their interiors that catch light, adding sparkle and textural interest. Crackled beads are usually transparent or translucent to maximize the effect of light passing through the cracks.

Translucent

Translucent beads allow some light to pass through them, so they appear to have inner glow. They often appear milky or cloudy in pale colorways. Beads with translucence come in faceted and polished finishes, as well as in every shape imaginable.

Hole Styles

Holes in beads vary widely. Those that have holes in the middle are referred to as *center-drilled* beads. *Side-drilled* beads have holes drilled across their short axis, sometimes at an offset angle. *Head-drilled* beads are often oblong with holes at their narrow ends.

●●● Strands

There are many different materials on which beads can be strung. While it is easy to generalize, it is important to understand how each strand material behaves so that you can choose the strand for your project. As a rule, it is best to string heavy beads on strands that are strong enough to support their weight without breaking. For lighter beads, strand material options broaden immeasurably.

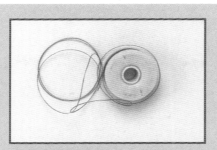

Silk Cord or Thread

Silk cord or thread is a strong natural material that is particularly suited to stringing pearls. Quite pliable, silk thread drapes well, but it must be knotted to be secured. Silk cord can fray, so condition it before stringing by pulling the thread through beeswax from the cut end toward the spool.

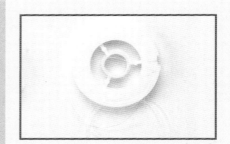

Plastic

A common plastic material used for beading is called transite. A strand of transite looks like transparent fishing line, and because it is nearly invisible, it is useful for stringing clear or pale-color beads. While quite strong, transite is not as strong as tigertail which has a reinforced metal core.

Braided

Braided wire is more flexible than ordinary wire and it is well suited to beading. Tigertail falls into this group; it has a braided stainless steel core coated with clear plastic so it is smooth to the touch. Transite comes in varying thicknesses – the thicker being stronger. Be sure to test fit the transite to your beads for easy stringing. To secure your beaded strand, use crimp beads or tubes. (Knotting transite is not recommended.) It is best to buy the same brand, matching the recommended sizes to achieve a sturdy closure.

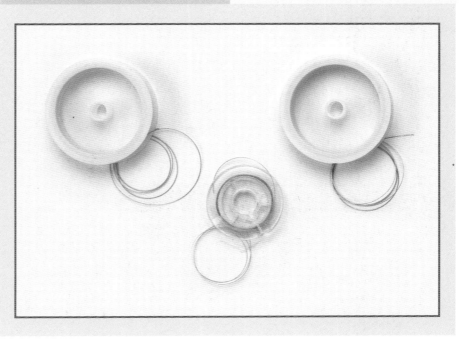

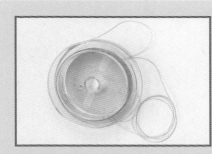

Elastic

Elastic line can be transparent and look like fishing line, but it's extremely "stretchy" and durable. It can be used for slip-on bracelets or for beads that would tear non-elastic strand material. It can be tied closed or crimped. It comes in a range of colors, making it appealing to beaders.

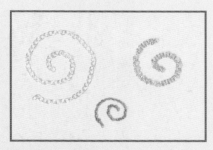

Chains

Chains are made by connecting links of wire together. They come in myriad link designs and finishes. They are used to support hanging decoration and to link parts of jewelry together. Sold by the inch, chains can be turned into jewelry by adding a clasp and beads on loops.

Wire

Wire is not used for stringing beads but rather to create findings such as loops and jump rings. It comes in different thicknesses called gauges. The larger the gauge, the thinner the diameter of the wire. In general the stiffness and strength of wire are determined by the metal used to make it.

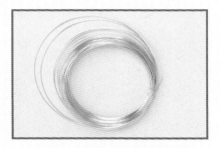

Sterling Silver: Sterling silver wire is made of silver that contains at least 92.5%, or 0.925 silver. The remaining percentage is copper. Silver is fairly soft but is easy to work with. It is easily polished to a high shine, and any scratches can be buffed out. Sterling silver is usually sold by weight, so if a thin gauge is used, it may not be too expensive to consider. Silver-plated wire can have a brass or copper core with the silver forming a thin layer on top. Some silver wire is tarnish resistant, having been treated by a chemical that retards oxidation.

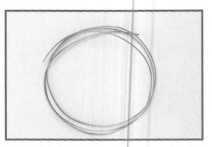

Gold Plated: Gold-plated wire does not tarnish, making it an attractive choice for jewelry. The wire has a core of base metal such as copper and a thin layer of gold plating, making the wire reasonable in price. Pliers can scratch off the plated layer, so it is important to handle the wire with care. Brass wire appears gold in color, but it will tarnish over time.

Memory Wire: Memory wire is a special kind of wire that bounces back to its original shape after it has been pulled out of shape. It is available in various gauges and diameters. Suited to bracelets and necklaces, the wire does not require clasps to secure it.

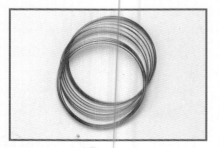

Findings

Findings, ranging from the basic to the exotic, are the essential components that finish a piece of jewelry. Findings can help suspend beads or keep them apart. They can connect design elements, stop beads from sliding off a strand, and fasten jewelry together. Here are the essential findings you will need.

Head Pins and Eye Pins

Head pins are short lengths of wire with either a ball, bar, disk, on one end. Eye pins have a hoop on one end. Both styles are threaded into bead holes and manipulated into loops using pliers. However, where head pins have a bead "stop," eye pins have an "eye" at the end through which another loop or pin can be threaded. Head and eye pins come in a variety of gauges and finishes.

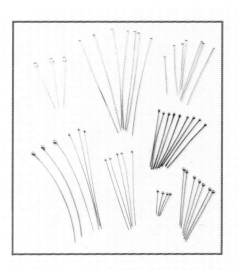

Jump Rings

Jump rings are very small metal hoops that connect jewelry-making components together. A jump ring might connect a beaded strand to a clasp, for example. Jump rings come in three styles: closed; open; and split. A closed jump ring has no split in it, so components must be secured using a knot or an open jump ring. An open jump ring has a split in the hoop so that loops or strands can be slipped on; the ring must be closed with two pairs of pliers. A split ring is a 1½-wind of stiff wire, much like a key ring, that must be forced open temporarily so looped beads can be slid on.

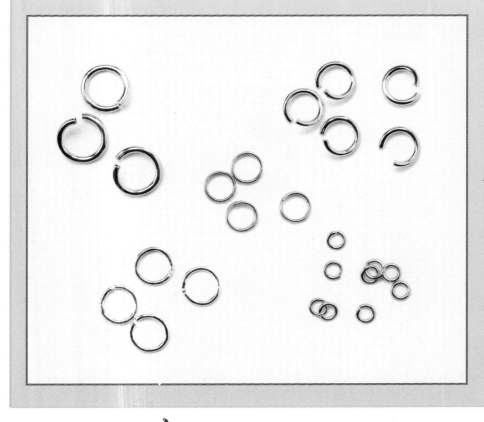

Spacer Beads

Spacer beads provide tiny spaces between beads so that the beads remain slightly separated and do not appear "squashed" together. Originally designed to be small and unobtrusive, spacer beads are now available with such interesting surface details that they become another design element with which to work when making jewelry. For example, daisy spacer beads have tiny balls around their edges creating the look of a tiny flower.

Clasps

Clasps come in a wide variety of styles and finishes. Mechanical clasps are generally the most reliable for necklaces, including the lobster-claw shape, ring, threaded barrel, or sliding snap. S-hook–, hook-and-ball–, and toggle clasps are easier to work. Toggle clasps are especially suited to bracelets because they are easy to connect using one hand. Magnetic clasps are an attractive option for lightweight necklaces, but they are not secure enough for use on bracelets, which often get bumped around with normal wear.

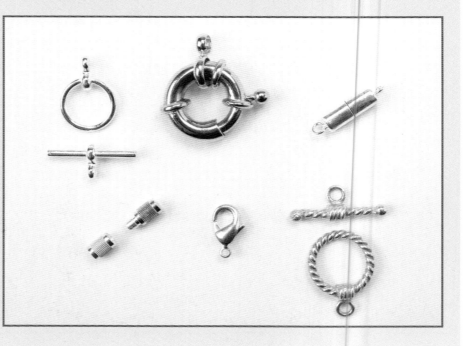

Hanging Drops

Metal drops are used to provide added weight to a dangling bead, like a pendant. They are available in a wide variety of shapes, sizes, and finishes. Used independently, they tend to draw the eye, adding design focus and interest.

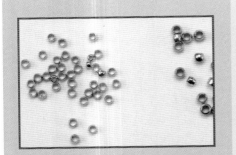

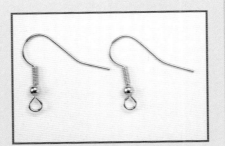

Crimp Fasteners

Crimp fasteners are small metal beads or tubes that are threaded on strands and squashed in place using a crimping tool. The crimping process secures the end of a strand of beads so that the beads won't slide off. Crimping using crimp beads and tubes can also secure the end loop in strand material.

Earring Hooks

Earrings require a clasp to secure them to the ear. One popular style is the fishhook ear wire used for pierced ears. Available in a wide variety of metals, the crook section of the hook is threaded through the ear, and the little loop at the end of the crook is hung with beads or other decorative elements.

Buttons

While not usually associated with beading, buttons can be used in place of beads. Because they have holes or back loops, they can be strung on a strand or affixed to a loop as long as their decorative faces can be seen. Buttons are available in an infinite variety of diameters, materials, finishes, and styles.

Basic Techniques

●●● Stringing Beads

Almost any material that is safe to handle and has a hole through which a strand can be threaded can be a bead. While the process of beading is straightforward in principle, there are occasions when special tools or techniques may save you time and effort. Here are a few professional secrets to make your beading experiences more fun and successful.

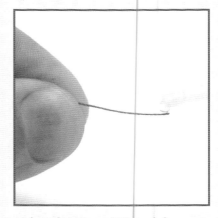

Using a Beading Needle

There are special beading needles that are thinner and longer than ordinary sewing needles. The appeal of using beading needles is that they allow many beads to be threaded on at a time, helping to avoid the cumbersome stringing of small beads that are often hard to handle. The eyes of beading needles are very small, so they are best suited to thin threads. For very tiny beads, use an embroidery needle with a blunt end. Pour the beads into a low, flat container, and guide the needle into the bead holes.

Using the Strand Material

Transform the thread on which small beads are strung into a "needle" by placing a ¼-in. dab of cyanoacrylate ("instant") glue at the end of the thread. Wait a couple of minutes for the glue to cure. Then use sharp thread cutters to cut across the dab of hardened glue to form a stiff tip (like the end a shoelace). This end can be threaded through the holes in small beads. Refresh the end of the thread when necessary. Nail polish can also be used to stiffen the thread, but it takes more time to dry.

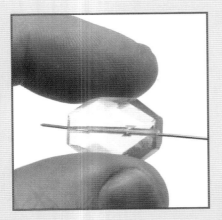

Using Your Fingers

Some strand material doesn't require any needle at all. If the strand material is fairly stiff, like wire, tigertail, or transite, you can easily thread the end of the strand into the beads as long the beads' holes are large enough. Oftentimes, the end of the strand frays or unravels, making it difficult to thread the material through the beads. In this case, apply glue or nail polish, as described in "Using the Strand Material" on this page, to remedy the problem as often as the strand material needs refreshing.

Making Your Own Beading "Needle"

It is easy to make your own "needle" to accommodate your beading needs.

1 Measure and cut a 6-in. length of 28-gauge or stiff beading wire.

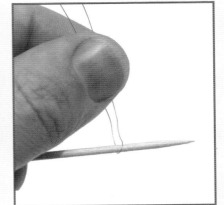

2 Fold the wire in half around a toothpick, as shown.

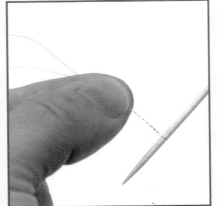

3 Twist the pair of wires between your fingers to form a straight spiral with a loop.

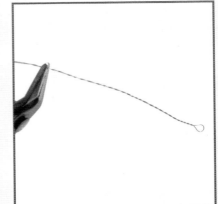

4 Slide the loop off the toothpick. Using wire cutters, snip the wires evenly across to make the "needle."

Using a Flexible Beading "Needle"

Another type of "needle" isn't really a needle at all. Flexible beading needles are actually very thin pieces of wire that are bent in half with a loop at one end. The loop is as large as ⅛ in. or more in diameter, so it can accommodate thicker strand

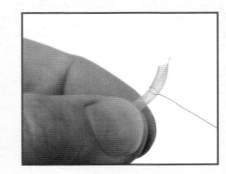

material, such as transite; heavier braided silk cord; and even narrow widths of gauze ribbon. The large loop collapses as the strand material is pulled through the bead hole, so the "needle" is very versatile. These "needles" can be purchased, or made by hand. Refer to "Make Your Own Beading Needle" page 123.

Restringing Small Beads

Small beads, such as seed beads, will frequently come in packages, vials, or hanks. When the beads are "hanked," they are pre-strung on single strands of cotton thread and knotted together at their ends. It is important to keep seed beads on the hank until you are ready to use them, but do not use the thread on which they came for your project. You will need to transfer the seed beads onto stronger strand material, as the cotton thread used to string them is unsuitable for use in jewelry-making. The process of re-threading the beads can be very tedious. The following steps will make the job easier.

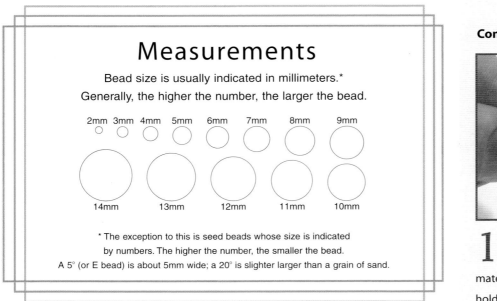

Measurements

Bead size is usually indicated in millimeters.*
Generally, the higher the number, the larger the bead.

2mm 3mm 4mm 5mm 6mm 7mm 8mm 9mm

14mm 13mm 12mm 11mm 10mm

* The exception to this is seed beads whose size is indicated
by numbers. The higher the number, the smaller the bead.
A 5° (or E bead) is about 5mm wide; a 20° is slighter larger than a grain of sand.

Connecting Strand Materials

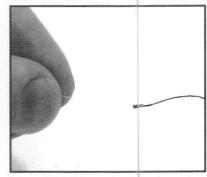

1 To string very tiny beads, glue the tip of the chosen strand material to the side of the thread that holds the beads, using "instant" glue.

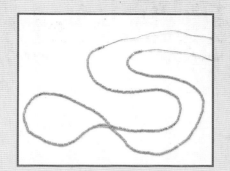

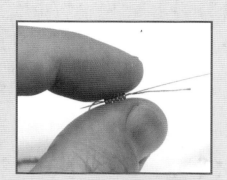

1 Lay the hank of beads on a flat surface. Identify the top knot or juncture where all the strands come together. Pick up one strand at the knot, and snip the thread using scissors. Carefully knot the end of the thread so the beads don't slip off.

2 Find the opposite end of the same strand by following it back to the top knot. Hold the beads near the top knot, and snip the strand from the hank using scissors.

3 While holding the end of the beaded strand between your thumb and index finger, insert a beading needle through 4 to 6 beads. Slide the beads onto the needle, then onto the strand on the needle. Continue to transfer the beads to the new strand material as before.

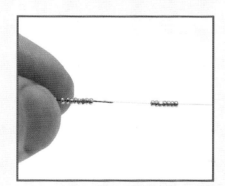

2 When the glue is dry, carefully slide seven beads over the glued section of strands to test the joint and to ensure that the remaining beads can pass over it.

3 Continue transferring the beads from the original thread to the new strand material until the required number of beads are threaded on the new strand material.

design tip

Mix seed beads in different finishes like glossy, transparent, and opalescent to create a design with high style.

••• Crimping Strand Material

Crimp beads

Crimp tubes

CRIMP BEADS AND CRIMP TUBES

Crimp beads and crimp tubes are used to create strong and durable "stops" on strand material to keep strung beads from slipping off. Each is a different shape, although both styles serve the same function. Crimp beads are round; crimp tubes are long. Made of metal, crimp beads and tubes come in varied finishes, such as silver, gold, and brass. They are made in different sizes, each suited to a different strand material, and are threaded onto a strand and squashed with a crimping tool. Crimping is faster and easier than hand-knotting which is used for the same purpose, especially by beginners.

In general, crimp beads and tubes need to correlate to both the thickness of the strand material and the diameter of the hole in the bead being strung. The bigger the beads, the heavier or sturdier the cord must be—and the larger the crimp beads. If you are not sure which to choose, look on the back of the packaging. If you buy the same brand for both the strand material and the crimp bead, the package information will indicate the right choices, and you will be assured an effective crimp.

THE CRIMPING PROCESS

While the process of crimping a crimp bead and a crimp tube is the same, it is important to note that the crimping tool is used twice. First the crimp bead (or tube) is squashed into a crescent shape, and then the crimp bead (or tube) is folded over. The finished crimp bead looks like a small knot, and the finished crimp tube looks like a narrow rectangle. The distinction is important in the ultimate appearance of the piece of jewelry, so consider it beforehand.

PREVENTING BEADS FROM BINDING

A finished crimp is like a hard metal "knot," and it is very

Using a crimp bead

1 Thread one end of the strand through the crimp bead, reinserting the end into the bead to form a loop.

unyielding when beads push against it. To prevent a strand of beads from binding and becoming inflexible, allow a small amount of space between the last bead strung and the crimp bead. For a standard 7-in. bracelet, allow about ⅟₁₆ in. between the last bead on the strand and the crimp bead. Instead of guessing, thread on a seed bead as a spacer; cover it with a tissue; and break it off the strand using pliers after you have attached the crimp bead. The missing seed bead will provide the needed ease.

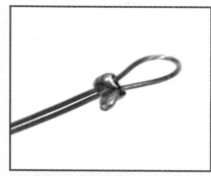

A malformed crimp bead

FIXING A CRIMP BEAD

Occasionally a crimp bead will be malformed, off-center on the strand, or folded over sloppily. As a first remedy, try squeezing the crimp again with the tip of the crimping tool. If this doesn't work, do not overwork the bad crimp. This can

Wire cutters removing the crimp bead

both weaken the metal and damage the strand material. Instead, begin again, removing the old crimp bead by carefully cutting along the side of the bead using wire snips or toenail clippers. Avoid cutting the strand material. The bad crimp bead will peel away easily.

2 Use the crescent-shaped space in the jaw of the crimping tool to squeeze the crimp bead.

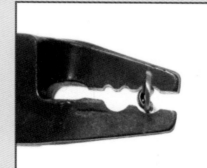

3 Use the round-shaped space in the jaw, clamping down on the bead to trap the strand material.

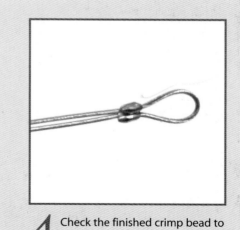

4 Check the finished crimp bead to make sure it traps the strand.

Note: the crimp bead will be round and compact.

●●● Working with Wire

Wire is a versatile material that provides sturdy and flexible connections between beads and on links and loops, depending on the chosen strand material. There are some basic guidelines for working with wire that will offer you consistently professional-looking results in your jewelry making. To begin, always wear eye protection when working with wire, as it can be unwieldy, and wire ends can go "flying" through the air when short ends are snipped. Put on safety goggles or glasses before you start work.

CUTTING WIRE

■ **Always use a pair of sharp wire cutters for the neatest cuts in wire.** Some needle-nose pliers have a wire-cutting slot near its pivot, and while it is suitable for occasional use, it is better to have a dedicated pair of wire cutters to produce superior cuts. Wire that is cut poorly can have undesirable bends, burrs, and snags.

■ **To cut wire of any kind, always cut straight across the wire.** Use the base of the pair of wire cutters rather than the tip for better leverage. Apply just enough firm pressure to make the cut. If the wire is not cut through cleanly, do not twist the pliers to force the cut, as this will only create sharp jags. Instead, release the pliers; reposition the jaws; and cut again. If this second effort doesn't work, it is possible that the blades of the wire cutter have become dull, so try to cut with a different part of the jaws. Sharpen or replace the wire cutter if these problems occur several times.

■ **To cut heavy or stiff wire,** use special caution because the wire may snap off when it's cut, sending a sharp piece flying. This is especially common when a short end of wire is cut. Be sure to wear eye protection to prevent injury. An easy way to keep short pieces from getting away is to carefully hold the end of the wire between your fingers while cutting the wire with the other hand. For longer lengths, hold the end with your hand, allowing the piece to drop in your hand when the wire is cut.

■ **Save your wire scraps, even the short pieces that are snipped off.** Some of the designs in this book may call for more wire in the materials list than is actually used. This is to make some allowance for the variations in the crafter's technique, and to accommodate the need for an extra tail of wire for leverage when bending wire. In all cases, save more-valuable wires, like sterling silver and gold plate, because they can be used to make jump rings or wire loops for another project.

■ **Smooth the jagged or rough ends of wire.** While thin wire measuring more than 22 or 24 gauge will generally require little or no smoothing, thicker wires may have sharp edges that require it. Use sandpaper or emery cloth to remove burrs from wire. 200- and 400-grit sand papers are best. Remember that the larger the number, the finer the grain of abrasive surface. When using emery cloth, smooth the jagged end of the wire as follows: lay the emery cloth on a flat surface, abrasive side up. Drag the end of the wire gently across the surface of the cloth at a 45-degree angle, rotating the wire to smooth the end evenly.

AVOIDING BREAKS

Metal wire must not be overworked by bending it back and forth. This weakens the metal, and the wire may eventually break. If a kink forms in the wire with which you are working, follow the recommendations below to fix the problem. If the kink cannot be fixed, restart with a fresh piece of wire.

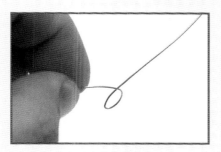

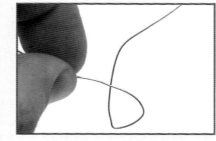

THE HISTORY OF A KINK

■ **A small kink often begins** as a small unwanted loop in the wire, an event common to wire crochet when a long tail of wire is pulled through a loop or wrapped around a bead.

■ **Don't pull the wire** in order to straighten the kink. That will only tighten it. Instead, use your fingers to open the loop of wire into a wide arc; then rotate the wire into a straight line.

■ **If a kink has formed,** flatten the section by gently squeezing it with the broad part of a pair of needle-nose pliers. Repeat, if necessary.

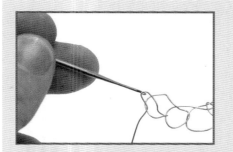

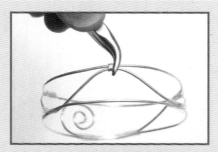

MANIPULATING THIN WIRE:

■ **Thin wire can be pulled** through narrow areas using a small crochet hook. To avoid damaging the wire and the hook, gently tug on the loop of wire, working it through slowly until the wire can be reached with your fingers.

■ **Hook-nose pliers can also be very helpful** in finishing a winding of wire when a pair of ordinary needle-nose pliers can't reach the wire or when extra leverage is needed. Avoid scratching the wire by pinching carefully it with the tip of the pliers.

design tip

Wire can play a strong role in the design of your jewelry. Use wire with a unique feature, like a square shape.

Making A Wire Loop

Making a wire loop using plain wire or a head-pin is an essential technique when creating pendant beads or swiveling connections between parts of a piece of jewelry.

A loop is composed of two parts: the round loop and the wrapped stem. You will need a pair of round-nose pliers to make the round loops. You will also need a pair of needle-nose pliers to crimp the wire tails into a wrapped stem. A pair of hook-nose pliers is also highly recommended because the offset tip provides extra leverage when you wind wires tightly into place, as you do when you are finishing the collar.

Loops can be made in fairly large diameters (7 to 10mm), depending on the gauge of the wire used. In general, a thicker-gauge wire is suitable for large loops, and thinner-gauge wire is better for small loops (2 to 4mm). When making any loop, consider the size and scale of the bead.

Making the Basic Wire Loop

1 Choose a ball-head pin whose length is at least 1 in. longer than the bead. Thread the plain end of the head pin into the bead, allowing the bead to slide down to the ball.

2 Firmly grip the wire stem emerging from the bead ³⁄₁₆ in. above the bead with round-nose pliers. Rotate the pliers 45 deg. in one direction to form a crook in the wire stem.

5 Remove the loop from the pliers. Use the widest part of the needle-nose pliers to grip the flat face of the loop to straighten it.

Note: to avoid scratching the surface, be careful not to slide the pliers across the wire.

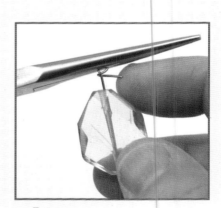

6 Continue to push the wire around the stem of the loop, using your fingers to form a collar, making sure the windings are close together.

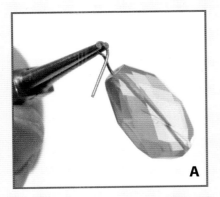

A

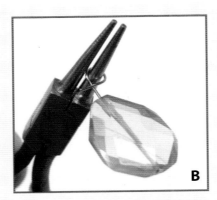

B

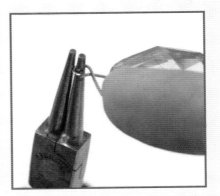

3 For a small loop, use the tips of round-nose pliers to grip the wire.

Note: the position on the pliers determines the diameter of the loop.

For a large loop, grip the wire near the bottom of the jaws of the round-nose pliers.

Note: the base of the pliers produces the largest loop.

4 Push the wire stem around the pliers using your fingertip, crossing over the crook in the wire.

7 Using wire cutters, snip off the excess wire when the windings are about two turns away from the bead. Smooth the wire end with an emery file.

8 To finish, gently squeeze the wire collar using hook-nose pliers.

Note: use caution to avoid cracking the bead.

design tip

Finishing the ends
of cut wire is important.
Smooth out rough cuts
using an emery file.

Making a Wrapped Loop

There is a special case in jewelry-making when a wrapped loop is preferable to—and more attractive than— the basic loop, and that is when you are making a loop for a bead with a head-drilled hole. Instead of winding the wire around the stem only, as in a regular loop, you wrap the wire around the tip of the bead so that it is conceals the bead hole and provides an appealing decorative element.

Note: it is a good idea to first practice the wrapped loop on a less-expensive bead.

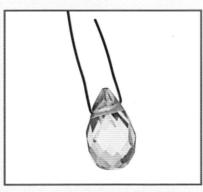

1 Cut a 2-in. length of 26-gauge wire. Thread it through the hole in the bead, leaving a ¾-in. tail. Bend both wires up toward the top of the bead.

Note: one wire will be shorter than the other.

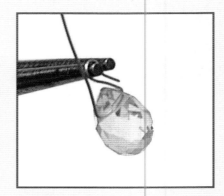

2 Grip the short wire using the round-nose pliers, and rotate the pliers to make a loop directly over the tip of the bead. Push the loop against the bead to make an "S" shape.

Making a Double Loop

There are times in jewelry-making when you want to add a beaded link to a chain or you want to connect the parts of a dangling earring in a decorative way. In these cases, a double-loop (or two-loop connection) can be used. First, choose a loop wire that is similar, if not identical, to the wire used in the chain. If the chain is sterling silver, use silver wire; if the chain is gold-plated, use gold-plated wire. Matching the loops to the chain gives the original piece a professional finish.

1 Thread a 2-in. length of 24-gauge wire through a pearl, centering it on the wire. Use round-nose pliers to make a 4mm loop, ⅛ in. from the pearl. For more details, see page 134.

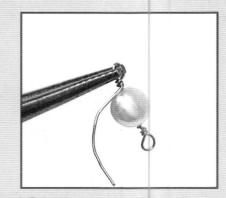

2 Repeat step 1 to make a 4mm loop, ⅛ in. from the pearl at the opposite side of the pearl, using pliers.

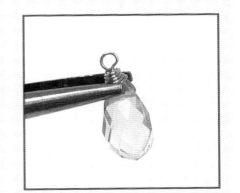

3 Hold the loop with the needle-nose pliers, and use your fingers to bring the long wire around the back of the bead, past the "S" loop, and around to the front of the bead.

4 Continue to wind the long wire around the wire stem and the bead, moving downward, to conceal the hole in the bead and complete the collar. Cut the wire end, using cutters.

5 For a neat finish, squeeze the wire collar with the tips of needle-nose pliers, being careful not to squeeze so hard as to break off the tip of the bead.

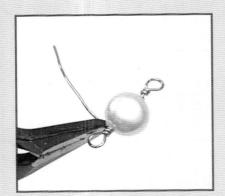

3 Use the tips of wire snips to cut off the excess wire at each loop. Smooth the ends of the wire using an emery file. Use needle-nose pliers to crimp the windings.

4 Snip out one link in the chain. Thread one end of an open jump ring through a loop on the pearl and a link in the chain. Close the ring.

5 Thread one end of a second open jump ring through the second loop on the pearl and the end link in the chain cut in step 4. Close the jump ring to connect the pearl to the chain.

Working with Jump Rings

OPEN JUMP RINGS

Open jump rings are particularly useful for joining components that have continuous loops that cannot be opened. The open jump ring is a simple hoop of metal with an open joint suitable to threading on looped beads. Jump rings need to be attached with care to ensure a secure closure, especially with wire that can slip between the joint or for heavy beads that can pull the jump ring out of shape, forcing it open.

design tip

Avoid pulling the ends of the ring apart sideways, as this can cause the ring to become distorted, making it difficult to match up its ends for a secure closure.

•

Avoid opening the jump ring any more than necessary because excess flexing can weaken the metal.

Attaching an Open Jump Ring

1 To create a connection using a jump ring, carefully open the ring by gripping it on one side of the opening with the flat part of a pair of needle-nose pliers.

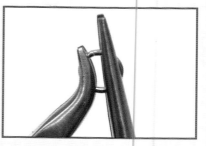

2 Grip the other half of the opening, using a pair of hook-nose pliers.

Making Jump Rings

Making your own jump rings is easy. Although ready-made jump rings are inexpensive, you may not be able to find a jump ring that is the right size or in the right wire thickness or finish. If you already have stiff wire that matches your project, you can use it to make jump rings for your project.

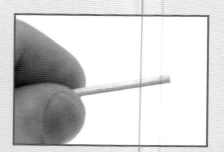

1 Find a rod-shaped item, like a toothpick, knitting needle, dowel, or any other item whose diameter equals the inside diameter of the ring you want to make.

Note: the diameter of the rod will determine the diameter of the jump ring.

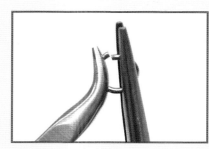

3 Carefully rotate the pair of hook-nose pliers toward you, pushing the needle-nose pliers away from you to move the ends of the ring out of plane.

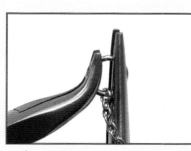

4 Keep the jump ring clamped in the needle-nose pliers, and slip on the strand. Close the jump ring by bringing the ends of the ring together, using the needle-nose and the hook-nose pliers.

5 Check to see that the closed jump ring does not have a gap between the ends of wire. If it does, use hook-nose pliers to squeeze the ring across its diameter and force the ends closed. Use caution to avoid distorting the shape of the ring.

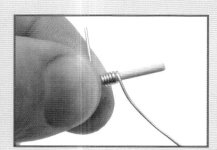

2 Hold the tail of a 4-in. length of wire against the rod, and wind the length around the rod as many times as the number of rings you need.

Note: even though a single jump ring requires only one wind of the wire, wind the wire two to three times around the toothpick to ensure that you make a complete jump ring.

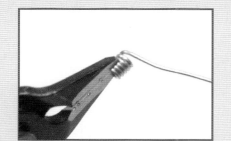

3 Carefully slide the toothpick out of the windings of wire to reveal a coil. Use the very tip of a pair of sharp wire cutters to cut through the wire coil along one side.

Note: this will cut the coil into individual split rings. If the wire ends are ragged, use emery cloth to smooth them.

4 Check to make sure the jump rings resemble little hoops with a split or opening.

Note: this opening allows the ring to be threaded through other loops or rings. Because the rings are so small, store them in a container with a transparent lid.

RESOURCES

Allcraft Jewelry Supply
135 W. 29th St.
Suite 402
New York, NY 10001
800-645-7124
www.allcraftonline.com
Professional tools, sterling wire

Artbeads.com
11901 137th Ave. Ct. KPN
Unit 100
Gig Harbor, WA 98329
253-857-3433
www.artbeads.com
beads, numerous findings

Beads On Fifth Inc
376 Fifth Ave.
New York, NY 10001
212-244-6616 and 244-6615
www.beadson5th.com
Better-than-usual selection of
hardware in sterling and gold fill;
heavy on Swarovski crystals

Beads World Inc
1384 Broadway
New York, NY 10018
212-302-1199
www.beadsworldusa.com
Loose and strung beads

Earthstone Co.
112 Harvard Ave. #54
Claremont, CA 91711
800-747-8088
www.earthstone.com
Great online pictures of various
shapes and stones

Fire Mountain Gems and Beads
One Fire Mountain Way
Grants Pass, OR 97526
800-423-2319
www.firemountaingems.com
Beads and findings

Fun 2 Bead
1028 Sixth Ave.
New York, NY 10018
212-302-3488
www.fun2bead.com
Loose and strung beads, findings

Genuine Ten Ten
1010 Sixth Ave.
New York, NY 10018
212-221-1173
Loose and strung beads, findings

Honey Beads
P.O. Box 8309
Fleming Island, FL 32006
904-607-4699
www.honeybeads.com
Very wide selection of bead styles

LouLou Button
69 W. 38th St.
New York, NY 10018
212-398-5498
Gold buttons, findings, and chains

Margola Import Corp.
48 W. 37th St.
New York, NY 10018
212-695-1115
www.margola.com
Strung and loose beads, seed beads

Master Wire Sculptor, Inc.
1600 Clay St.
Vicksburg, MS 39183
www.wire-sculpture.com
Packed with materials and advice

Metalliferous
34 W. 46th St.
2nd Floor
New York, NY 10036
212-944-0909
www.metalliferous.com
Metal findings; wire; chain;
bangles; good source for tools

Michaels Stores, Inc.
8000 Bent Branch Dr.
Irving, TX 75063
800-642-4235
www.michaels.com
National chain of craft supplies,
including comprehensive beading
section with beads, tools, and wire

New Age Enterprises
P.O. Box 14492
Tumwater, WA 98511
360-705-3299
www.gembeads.com
Not a wide selection but has
unusual items

New York Beads
1026 Sixth Ave.
New York, NY 10018
212-382-2994
Loose and strung beads

Tinsel Trading
47 W. 38th St.
New York, NY 10018
212-730-1030
www.tinseltrading.com
Cords and ribbons, trims, buttons,
and beads

Toho Shoji
990 Sixth Ave.
New York, NY 10018
212-868-7466
www.tohoshojiny.com
Beads, findings, and chains

Trim World USA
49 W. 37th St.
New York, NY 10018
212-391-1046
Strung and loose beads, and
gold and silver findings

INDEX

If you like **Glamorous Beaded Jewelry**

take a look at other titles in our Home Arts Series
Knit Style and **The Decorated Bag**

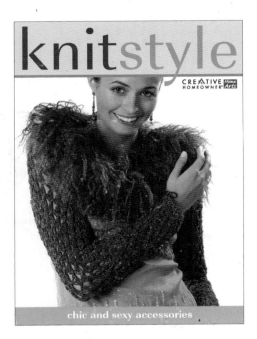

Knit Style is a collection of 25 fabulous accessories for every occasion, each original item knitted in today's most popular yarns, like fun fur, chenille, and chunky, and shown in orginal full-color photographs.

- Over 125 beautiful full-color photographs, instructional illustrations, and diagrams of all the gorgeous knitted accessories
- Geared to the beginner and veteran knitter alike, the collection includes such fashion favorites as a shrug with faux fur collar and cuffs, an extra-chunky poncho, and a delicate capelet with bell sleeves.
- Clear and concise step-by-step patterns and professional knitting tips, together with special sections that show the essential techniques and list the best sources for knitting supplies
- An easel-back, spiral-bound book that allows "hands free" access to the information on each beautifully illustrated page

Knit Style
ISBN: 1-58011-305-2
UPC: 0-78585-11305-7
CH Book #265142
128 pages, 8" x 10⁷/₈"
$19.95 US / $24.95 CAN

The Decorated Bag is a fun and stylish collection of 50 bags that are decorated using embellishments such as sparkling rhinestones, pom-poms, jewelry, faux fur, and ribbons and trims of every description.

- Over 175 original full-color images and step-by-step photographs accompanied by directions for all of the decorative techniques explained in user-friendly language, and suited to all skill levels, especially the beginner
- 25 beautiful and stylish bags PLUS another 25 design variations, including patterns for making the clutch-, pull-string-, and tote-style designs from scratch
- Author, Genevieve A. Sterbenz, is a well-known designer and television personality.

The Decorated Bag
ISBN: 1-58011-296-X
UPC: 0-78585-11296-8
CH Book # 265138
144 pages, 8¹/₂" x 9¹/₂"
$19.95 US / $24.95 CAN

Look for these and other fine **Creative Homeowner** books wherever books are sold.
For more information and to order direct, go to **www.creativehomeowner.com**